THE BRUISED REED

THE BRUISED REED

Richard Sibbes

THE BANNER OF TRUTH TRUST

THE BANNER OF TRUTH TRUST
3 Murrayfield Road, Edinburgh EH12 6EL
P.O. Box 621, Carlisle, Pennsylvania 17013, USA

*

First published 1630
First Banner of Truth revised edition 1998
ISBN 0 85151 740 4

*

Typeset in 10½/12pt Plantin
at The Banner of Truth Trust, Edinburgh
Printed and bound in Finland
by WSOY

Contents

Publishers' Foreword

'Our books may come to be seen where ourselves shall never be heard. These may preach where the author cannot, and (which is more) when he is not.' This prediction by one of the great Puritans has had many fulfilments. An ungodly Welsh clergyman, shopping at a fair in the eighteenth century, bought an article which happened to be wrapped in a page torn from an old Puritan folio. The reading of that one page led to his sound conversion. As Luther said, 'Satan hates the use of pens,' and never were pens more powerfully wielded in the cause of God than by the Puritan divines of the seventeenth century. Nor have their books outlived their usefulness. Although the original volumes are worn with age, the truths found in them are as fresh as the new formats in which they are now appearing.

There is no better introduction to the Puritans than the writings of Richard Sibbes, who is, in many ways, a typical Puritan. 'Sibbes never wastes the student's time,' wrote C. H. Spurgeon, 'he scatters pearls and diamonds with both hands.'

The facts concerning Sibbes' life can be briefly stated (there is a full account in Volume 1 of the Banner of Truth Trust edition of his *Works*). He was born at Tostock, Suffolk, in 1577 and went to school at Bury St Edmunds. His father intended Richard to follow his own trade as a wheelwright, but, with the help of friends, he went up to

St John's College, Cambridge, in 1595. Here he was converted under the powerful preaching of Paul Bayne, the successor of William Perkins in the pulpit of Great St Andrew's Church. After earning his B.D. in 1610, he was appointed a lecturer at Holy Trinity Church, Cambridge. He was removed from this post five years later, however, because of his Puritan tendencies. Through the influence of powerful friends, he was chosen to be the preacher at Gray's Inn, London, in 1617, and remained there till 1626. In that year he returned to Cambridge as Master of St Catherine's Hall, and later returned to Holy Trinity, this time as its vicar. He was granted a Doctorate in Divinity in 1627, and was thereafter frequently referred to as 'the heavenly Doctor Sibbes', on account of both the matter and the manner of his preaching. He continued to exercise his ministry, at Gray's Inn, London, as well as at Holy Trinity, Cambridge, while also remaining Master of St Catherine's, until his death on 6 July 1635, at the age of 58. Of him Izaak Walton later wrote: 'Of this blest man, let this just praise be given: heaven was in him, before he was in heaven.'

'The Lord took him away,' wrote a contemporary, 'that his eyes might not see the great evils which were about to break out upon the land.' These great evils came to a head in the Civil War of the 1640s. Behind that event lay a movement away from the doctrines and practices of the Reformation on the part of a powerful faction in the Church of England, headed by William Laud, Archbishop of Canterbury, and backed by royal favour. It was the Puritans who stood together to meet these inroads. To them moderation in maintaining the truth of God's Word was but sinful lukewarmness. 'A curse lies upon those', said Sibbes, 'that, when the truth suffers, have not a word to defend it.' For his boldness, Sibbes was reprimanded in 1627, and in 1632, along with eleven other Puritan ministers, he was sentenced to banishment. The sentence was never carried out, but Sibbes lived to see many of his dear friends, such as Samuel Ward, Thomas Goodwin, John Cotton, Thomas Hooker and others, imprisoned or forced into exile in Holland or New England. Concerning the final issue of this conflict Sibbes was in no doubt. Gardiner, in his *History of the Puritan Revolution,* writes, 'Sibbes is distinguished by his triumphant confidence . . . [while] even Laud and Wentworth acknowledged to themselves that the chances were against them. Eliot in his prison, and Sibbes in his pulpit, are jubilant with exultation.'

Sibbes himself says:

> A Christian is an impregnable person. He is a person that never can be conquered. Emmanuel became man to make the church and every Christian to be one with him. Christ's nature is out of danger of all that is hurtful. The sun shall not shine, the wind shall not blow, to the church's hurt. For the church's Head ruleth over all things and hath all things in subjection. Therefore let all the enemies consult together, this king and that power, there is a counsel in heaven which will disturb and dash all their counsels. Emmanuel in heaven laugheth them to scorn. And as Luther said, 'Shall we weep and cry when God laugheth?'

Since its first publication in 1630, *The Bruised Reed* has been remarkably fruitful as a source of spiritual help and comfort. Richard Baxter records: 'A poor pedlar came to the door . . . and my father bought of him Sibb's *Bruised Reed* . . . It suited my state . . . and gave me a livelier apprehension of the mystery of redemption and how much I was beholden to Jesus Christ . . . Without any means but books was God pleased to resolve me to himself.' Such testimonies could be multiplied. Speaking of the preacher's need to suit his reading to the varying conditions he finds within, Dr Martyn Lloyd-Jones says in his *Preaching and Preachers:*

> You will find, I think, in general that the Puritans are almost invariably helpful . . . I shall never cease to be grateful to one of them called Richard Sibbes who was balm to my soul at a period in my life when I was overworked and badly overtired, and therefore subject in an unusual manner to the onslaughts of the devil. In that state and condition . . . what you need is some gentle, tender treatment for your soul. I found at that time that Richard Sibbes, who was known in London in the early seventeenth century as 'the heavenly Doctor Sibbes', was an unfailing remedy. His books *The Bruised Reed* and *The Soul's Conflict* quietened, soothed, comforted, encouraged and healed me.

The complete works of Sibbes were published in seven volumes in the Nichol Series between 1862 and 1864, and again by the Banner of Truth Trust, between 1973 and 1982. The present book is taken from the first volume in that series and is the first of Sibbes' writings to be published separately in the present series. Some of the language and punctuation of the earlier edition have been modernized and headings have been introduced with the intention of making the work more accessible to present-day readers.

Sibbes once said to Thomas Goodwin, 'Young man, if ever you would do good, you must preach the gospel and the free grace of God in Christ Jesus.' *The Bruised Reed* shows us how Sibbes himself did this. May he, by this work, though dead, yet speak (*Heb.* 11:4), both to readers who are already familiar with his writings and to those who have still to discover him.

January 1998

1. *The Reed and the Bruising*

The prophet Isaiah, being lifted up and carried with the wing of a prophetical spirit, passes over all the time between him and the appearing of Jesus Christ in the flesh. Seeing with the eye of prophecy, and with the eye of faith, Christ as present, he presents him, in the name of God, to the spiritual eye of others, in these words: 'Behold my servant, whom I uphold; mine elect, in whom my soul delighteth; I have put my spirit upon him: he shall bring forth judgment to the Gentiles. He shall not cry, nor lift up, nor cause his voice to be heard in the street. A bruised reed shall he not break, and the smoking flax shall he not quench: he shall bring forth judgment unto truth' (*Isa.* 42:1–3). These words are alleged by Matthew as fulfilled now in Christ (*Matt.* 12:18–20). In them are propounded, first, the calling of Christ to his office; secondly, the manner in which he carries it out.

CHRIST'S CALLING

God calls him here his servant. Christ was God's servant in the greatest piece of service that ever was, a chosen and a choice servant who did and suffered all by commission from the Father. In this we may see the sweet love of God to us, in that he counts the work of our salvation by Christ his greatest service, and in that he will put his only beloved Son to that service. He might well prefix it with 'Behold' to raise up our thoughts to the highest pitch of attention and admiration. In time of temptation, apprehensive consciences look so much to the present trouble they are in that they need to be roused up to behold him in whom they may find rest for their distressed souls. In temptations it is safest to behold nothing but Christ the true brazen serpent, the true 'Lamb of God that taketh away the sin of the world' (*John* 1:29). This saving object has a special influence of comfort to the soul, especially if we look not only on Christ, but upon the Father's authority and love in him. For in all that Christ did and suffered as Mediator, we must see God in him reconciling the world unto himself (*2 Cor.* 5:19).

What a support to our faith is this, that God the Father, the party offended by our sins, is so well pleased with the work of redemption! And what a comfort is this, that, seeing God's love rests on Christ, as well pleased in him, we may gather that he is as well pleased with us, if we be in Christ! For his love rests in a whole Christ, in Christ mystical, as well as Christ natural, because he loves him and us with one love. Let us, therefore, embrace Christ, and in him God's love, and build our faith safely on such a Saviour that is furnished with so high a commission.

See here, for our comfort, a sweet agreement of all three persons: the Father gives a commission to Christ; the Spirit furnishes and sanctifies to it, and Christ himself executes the office of a Mediator. Our redemption is founded upon the joint agreement of all three persons of the Trinity.

HOW CHRIST PURSUES HIS CALLING

This is here said to be done modestly, without making a noise, or raising dust by any pompous coming, as princes are accustomed to do. 'His voice shall not be heard.' His voice indeed was heard, but what voice? 'Come unto me, all ye that labour and are heavy laden' (*Matt.* 11:28). He cried, but how? 'Ho, every one that thirsteth, come ye to the waters' (*Isa.* 55:1). And as his coming was modest, so it was mild, which is set down in these words: 'A bruised reed shall he not break, and smoking flax shall he not quench.'

We see, therefore, that the condition of those with whom he was to deal was that they were bruised reeds and smoking flax; not trees, but reeds; and not whole, but bruised reeds. The church is compared to weak things: to a dove amongst the fowls; to a vine amongst the plants; to sheep amongst the beasts; to a woman, which is the weaker vessel.

God's children are bruised reeds before their conversion and oftentimes after. Before conversion all (except such as, being brought up in the church, God has delighted to show himself gracious to from their childhood) are bruised reeds, yet in different degrees, as God sees fit. And as there are differences with regard to temperament, gifts and manner of life, so there are in God's intention to use men in the time to come; for usually he empties such of themselves, and makes them nothing, before he will use them in any great services.

WHAT IT IS TO BE BRUISED

The bruised reed is a man that for the most part is in some misery, as those were that came to Christ for help, and by misery he is brought to see sin as the cause of it, for, whatever pretences sin makes, they come to an end when we are bruised and broken. He is sensible of sin and misery, even unto bruising; and, seeing no help in himself, is carried with restless desire to have supply from another, with some hope, which a little raises him out of himself to Christ, though he dare not claim any present interest of mercy. This spark of hope being opposed by doubtings and fears rising from corruption makes him as smoking flax; so that both these together, a *bruised* reed and *smoking* flax, make up the state of a poor distressed man. This is such an one as our Saviour Christ terms 'poor in spirit' (*Matt.* 5:3), who sees his wants, and also sees himself indebted to divine justice. He has no means of supply from himself or the creature, and thereupon mourns, and, upon some hope of mercy from the promise and examples of those that have obtained mercy, is stirred up to hunger and thirst after it.

THE GOOD EFFECTS OF BRUISING

This bruising is required before conversion that so the Spirit may make way for himself into the heart by levelling all proud, high thoughts, and that we may understand ourselves to be what indeed we are by nature. We love to wander from ourselves and to be strangers at home, till God bruises us by one cross or other, and then we 'begin to think', and come home to ourselves with the prodigal (*Luke* 15:17). It is a very hard thing to bring a dull and an evasive heart to cry with feeling for mercy. Our hearts, like criminals, until they be beaten from all evasions, never cry for the mercy of the Judge.

Again, this bruising makes us set a high price upon Christ. Then the gospel becomes the gospel indeed; then the fig-leaves of morality will do us no good. And it makes us more thankful, and, from thankfulness, more fruitful in our lives; for what makes many so cold and barren, but that bruising for sin never endeared God's grace to them?

Likewise this dealing of God establishes us the more in his ways, having had knocks and bruisings in our own ways. This is often the cause of relapses and apostasy, because men never smarted for sin at the first; they were not long enough under the lash of the law. Hence this inferior work of the Spirit in bringing down high thoughts (*2 Cor.* 10:5) is necessary before conversion. And, for the most part, the Holy Spirit, to further the work of conviction, joins with it some affliction, which, when sanctified, has a healing and purging power.

After conversion we need bruising so that reeds may know themselves to be reeds, and not oaks. Even reeds need bruising, by reason of the remainder of pride in our nature, and to let us see that we live by mercy. Such bruising may help weaker Christians not to be too much discouraged, when they see stronger ones shaken and bruised. Thus Peter was bruised when he wept bitterly (*Matt.* 26:75). This reed, till he met with this bruise, had more wind in him than pith when he said, 'Though all forsake thee, I will not' (*Matt.* 26:33). The people of God cannot be without these examples. The heroic deeds of those great worthies do not comfort the church so much as their falls and bruises do. Thus David was bruised until he came to a free confession, without guile of spirit (*Psa.* 32:3–5); nay, his sorrows did rise in his own feeling unto the exquisite pain of breaking of bones (*Psa.* 51:8). Thus Hezekiah complains that God had 'broken his bones' as a lion (*Isa.* 38:13). Thus the chosen vessel Paul needed the messenger of Satan to buffet him lest he should be lifted up above measure (2 *Cor.* 12:7).

Hence we learn that we must not pass too harsh judgment upon ourselves or others when God exercises us with bruising upon bruising. There must be a conformity to our head, Christ, who 'was bruised for us' (*Isa.* 53:5) that we may know how much we are bound unto him.

Ungodly spirits, ignorant of God's ways in bringing his children to heaven, censure broken-hearted Christians as miserable persons, whereas God is doing a gracious, good work with them. It is no easy matter to bring a man from nature to grace, and from grace to glory, so unyielding and intractable are our hearts.

2. Christ Will Not Break the Bruised Reed

In pursuing his calling, Christ will not break the bruised reed, nor quench the smoking flax, in which more is meant than spoken, for he will not only not break nor quench, but he will cherish those with whom he so deals.

CHRIST'S DEALINGS WITH THE BRUISED REED

Physicians, though they put their patients to much pain, will not destroy nature, but raise it up by degrees. Surgeons will lance and cut, but not dismember. A mother who has a sick and self-willed child will not therefore cast it away. And shall there be more mercy in the stream than in the spring? Shall we think there is more mercy in ourselves than in God, who plants the affection of mercy in us?

But for further declaration of Christ's mercy to all bruised reeds, consider the comfortable relationships he has taken upon himself of husband, shepherd and brother, which he will discharge to the utmost. Shall others by his grace fulfil what he calls them unto, and not he who, out of his love, has taken upon him these relationships, so thoroughly founded upon his Father's assignment, and his own voluntary undertaking? Consider the names he has borrowed from the mildest creatures, such as lamb and hen, to show his tender care. Consider his very name Jesus, a Saviour, given him by God himself. Consider his office answerable to his name, which is that he should 'bind up the broken-hearted' (*Isa.* 61:1). At his baptism the Holy Ghost rested on him in the shape of a dove, to show that he should be a dove-like, gentle Mediator.

See the gracious way he executes his offices. As a prophet, he came with blessing in his mouth, 'Blessed are the poor in spirit' (*Matt.* 5:3), and invited those to come to him whose hearts suggested most exceptions against themselves, 'Come unto me, all ye that labour and are heavy laden' (*Matt.* 11:28). How did his heart yearn when he saw the people 'as sheep having no shepherd' (*Matt.* 9:36)! He never turned any back again that came to him, though some went away of themselves. He came to die as a priest for his enemies. In the days of his flesh he dictated a form of prayer unto his disciples, and put petitions unto God into their mouths, and his Spirit to intercede in their hearts. He shed tears for those that shed his blood, and now he makes intercession in heaven for weak Christians, standing between them and God's anger. He is a meek king; he will admit mourners into his presence, a king of poor and afflicted persons. As he has beams of majesty, so he has a heart of mercy and compassion. He is the prince of peace (*Isa.* 9:6). Why was he tempted, but that he might 'succour them that are tempted' (*Heb.* 2:18)? What mercy may we not expect from so gracious a Mediator (*1 Tim.* 2:5) who took our nature upon him that he might be gracious? He is a physician good at all diseases, especially at the binding up of a broken heart. He died that he might heal our souls with a plaster of his own blood, and by that death save us, which we were the procurers of ourselves, by our own sins. And has he not the same heart in heaven? 'Saul, Saul, why persecutest thou me?' cried the Head in heaven, when the foot on earth was trodden on (*Acts* 9:4). His advancement has not made him forget his own flesh. Though it has freed him from passion, yet not from compassion towards us. The lion of the tribe of Judah will only tear in pieces those that 'will not have him rule over them' (*Luke* 19:14). He will not show his strength against those who prostrate themselves before him.

FOR OURSELVES

1. What should we learn from this, but to 'come boldly to the throne of grace' (*Heb.* 4:16) in all our grievances? Shall our sins discourage us, when he appears there only for sinners? Are you bruised? Be of good comfort, he calls you. Conceal not your wounds, open all before him and take not Satan's counsel. Go to Christ, although trembling, as the poor woman who said, 'If I may but touch his garment' (*Matt.* 9:21). We shall be healed and have a gracious answer. Go boldly to God in our flesh; he is flesh of our flesh, and bone of our bone for this reason, that we might go boldly to him. Never fear to go to God, since we have such a Mediator with him, who is not only our friend but our brother and husband. Well might the angel proclaim from heaven, 'Behold, I bring you good tidings of great joy' (*Luke* 2:10). Well might the apostle stir us up to 'rejoice in the Lord alway: and again I say, Rejoice' (*Phil.* 4:4). Paul was well advised upon what grounds he did it. Peace and joy are two main fruits of Christ's kingdom. Let the world be as it will, if we cannot rejoice in the world, yet we may rejoice in the Lord. His presence makes any condition comfortable. 'Be not afraid,' says he to his disciples, when they were afraid, as if they had seen

a ghost, 'It is I' (*Matt.* 14:27), as if there were no cause of fear where he was present.

2. Let this support us when we feel ourselves bruised. Christ's way is first to wound, then to heal. No sound, whole soul shall ever enter into heaven. Think when in temptation, Christ was tempted for me; according to my trials will be my graces and comforts. If Christ be so merciful as not to break me, I will not break myself by despair, nor yield myself over to the roaring lion, Satan, to break me in pieces.

3. See the contrary disposition of Christ on the one hand and Satan and his instruments on the other. Satan sets upon us when we are weakest, as Simeon and Levi upon the Shechemites, 'when they were sore' (*Gen.* 34:25), but Christ will make up in us all the breaches which sin and Satan have made. He 'binds up the broken-hearted' (*Isa.* 61:1). As a mother is tenderest to the most diseased and weakest child, so does Christ most mercifully incline to the weakest. Likewise he puts an instinct into the weakest things to rely upon something stronger than themselves for support. The vine stays itself upon the elm, and the weakest creatures often have the strongest shelters. The consciousness of the church's weakness makes her willing to lean on her beloved, and to hide herself under his wing.

WHO ARE THE BRUISED REEDS?

But how shall we know whether we are such as may expect mercy?

Answer: (1) By *the bruised* here is not meant those that are brought low only by crosses, but such as, by them, are brought to see their sin, which bruises most of all. When conscience is under the guilt of sin, then every judgment brings a report of God's anger to the soul, and all lesser troubles run into this great trouble of conscience for sin. As all corrupt humours run to the diseased and bruised part of the body, and as every creditor falls upon the debtor when he is once arrested, so when conscience is once awakened, all former sins and present crosses join together to make the bruise the more painful. Now, he that is thus bruised will be content with nothing but with mercy from him who has bruised him. He has wounded, and he must heal (*Hos.* 6:1). The Lord who has bruised me deservedly for my sins must bind up my heart again. (2) Again, a man truly bruised judges sin the greatest evil, and the favour of God the greatest good. (3) He would rather hear of mercy than of a kingdom. (4) He has poor opinions of himself, and thinks that he is not worth the earth he treads on. (5) Towards others he is not censorious, as being taken up at home, but is full of sympathy and compassion to those who are under God's hand. (6) He thinks that those who walk in the comforts of God's Spirit are the happiest men in the world. (7) He trembles at the Word of God (*Isa.* 66:2), and honours the very feet of those blessed instruments that bring peace unto him (*Rom.* 10:15). (8) He is more taken up with the inward exercises of a broken heart than with formality, and is yet careful to use all sanctified means to convey comfort.

But how shall we come to this state of mind?
Answer: First, we must conceive of bruising either as a state into which God brings us, or as a duty to be performed by us. Both are here meant. We must join with God in bruising ourselves. When he humbles us, let us humble ourselves, and not stand out against him, for then he will redouble his strokes. Let us justify Christ in all his chastisements, knowing that all his dealing towards us is to cause us to return into our own hearts. His work in

bruising tends to our work in bruising ourselves. Let us lament our own perversity, and say: Lord, what a heart have I that needs all this, that none of this could be spared! We must lay siege to the hardness of our own hearts, and aggravate sin all we can. We must look on Christ, who was bruised for us, look on him whom we have pierced with our sins. But all directions will not prevail, unless God by his Spirit convinces us deeply, setting our sins before us, and driving us to a standstill. Then we will cry out for mercy. Conviction will breed contrition, and this leads to humiliation. Therefore desire God that he would bring a clear and a strong light into all the corners of our souls, and accompany it with a spirit of power to lay our hearts low.

A set measure of bruising of ourselves cannot be prescribed, but it must be so far as (1) that we may prize Christ above all, and see that a Saviour must be had; and (2) that we reform that which is amiss, though it be to the cutting off of our right hand, or pulling out of our right eye. There is a dangerous slighting of the work of humiliation, some alleging this for a pretence for their casual dealing with their own hearts, that Christ will not break the bruised reed; but such must know that every sudden terror and short grief is not that which makes us bruised reeds; not a little 'bowing down our heads like a bulrush' (*Isa.* 58:5), but a working our hearts to such a grief as will make sin more odious unto us than punishment, until we offer a 'holy violence' against it. Else, favouring ourselves, we make work for God to bruise us, and for sharp repentance afterwards. It is dangerous, I confess, in some cases, with some spirits, to press too much and too long this bruising, because they may die under the wound and burden before they be raised up again. Therefore it is good in mixed assemblies to mingle comfort that every soul may have its due portion. But if we have this for a foundation truth, that there is more mercy in Christ than sin in us, there can be no danger in thorough dealing. It is better to go bruised to heaven than sound to hell. Therefore let us not take off ourselves too soon, nor pull off the plaster before the cure be wrought, but keep ourselves under this work till sin be the sourest, and Christ the sweetest, of all things. And when God's hand is upon us in any way, it is good to divert our sorrow for other things to the root of all, which is sin. Let our grief run most in that channel, that as sin bred grief, so grief may consume sin.

But are we not bruised unless we grieve more for sin than we do for punishment ?
Answer: Sometimes our grief from outward grievances may lie heavier upon the soul than grief for God's displeasure, because, in such cases, the grief works upon the whole man, both outward and inward, and has nothing to support it, but a little spark of faith. This faith, by reason of the violent impression of the grievance, is suspended in the exercises of it. This is most felt in sudden distresses which come upon the soul as a torrent or land-flood, and especially in bodily sicknesses which, by reason of the sympathy between the soul and the body, work upon the soul so far as to hinder not only the spiritual, but often the natural acts. Therefore, James wishes us in affliction to pray ourselves, but in case of sickness to 'send for the elders' (*James* 5:14). These may, as those in the Gospels, offer up to God in their prayers the sick person who is unable to present his own case. Hereupon God admits of such a plea from the sharpness and bitterness of the grievance, as in David (*Psa.* 6). The Lord knows our frame; he remembers that we are but dust (*Psa.* 103:14), that our strength is not the strength of steel.

This is a branch of his faithfulness to us as his creatures, whence he is called 'a faithful Creator' (*1 Pet.* 4:19). 'God is faithful, who will not suffer you to be tempted above that ye are able' (*1 Cor.* 10:13). There were certain commandments which the Jews called the hedges of the law. So as to fence men off from cruelty, God commanded that they should not take the dam with the young, nor 'seethe a kid in his mother's milk' (*Exod.* 23:19), nor 'muzzle the mouth of the ox' (*1 Cor.* 9:9). Does God take care of beasts, and not of his more noble creature? And therefore we ought to judge charitably of the complaints of God's people which are wrung from them in such cases. Job had the esteem with God of a patient man, notwithstanding those passionate complaints. Faith overborne for the present will gain ground again; and grief for sin, although it come short of grief for misery in terms of violence, yet it goes beyond it in constancy; as a running stream fed with a spring holds out, when a sudden swelling brook fails.

For the concluding of this point, and our encouragement to a thorough work of bruising, and patience under God's bruising of us, let all know that none are fitter for comfort than those that think themselves furthest off. Men, for the most part, are not lost enough in their own feeling for a Saviour. A holy despair in ourselves is the ground of true hope. In God the fatherless find mercy (*Hos.* 14:3); if men were more fatherless, they should feel more God's fatherly affection from heaven, for the God who dwells in the highest heavens dwells likewise in the lowest soul (*Isa.* 57:15). Christ's sheep are weak sheep, and lacking in something or other; he therefore applies himself to the necessities of every sheep. He seeks that which was lost, and brings again that which was driven out of the way, and binds up that which was broken, and strengthens the weak (*Ezek.* 34:16). His tenderest care is over the weakest. The lambs he carries in his bosom (*Isa.* 40:11). He says to Peter, 'Feed my lambs' (*John* 21:15). He was most familiar and open to troubled souls. How careful he was that Peter and the rest of the apostles should not be too much dejected after his resurrection! 'Go your way, tell his disciples and Peter' (*Mark* 16:7). Christ knew that guilt of their unkindness in leaving of him had dejected their spirits. How gently did he endure the unbelief of Thomas and stooped so far unto his weakness, as to suffer him to thrust his hand into his side.

3. *The Smoking Flax*

In pursuing his calling, Christ will not quench the smoking flax, or wick, but will blow it up till it flames. In smoking flax there is but a little light, and that weak, as being unable to flame, and that little mixed with smoke. The observations from this are that, in God's children, especially in their first conversion, there is but a little measure of grace, and that little mixed with much corruption, which, as smoke, is offensive; but that Christ will not quench this smoking flax.

GRACE IS LITTLE AT FIRST

There are several ages in Christians, some babes, some young men. Faith may be as 'a grain of mustard seed' (*Matt.* 17:20). Nothing so little as grace at first, and nothing more glorious afterward. Things of greatest perfection are longest in coming to their growth. Man, the most perfect creature, comes to perfection by little and little; worthless things, as mushrooms and the like, like Jonah's gourd, soon spring up, and soon vanish. A new creature is the most excellent creature in all the world, therefore it grows up by degrees. We see in nature that a mighty oak rises from an acorn. It is with a Christian as it was with Christ, who sprang out of the dead stock of Jesse, out of David's family (*Isa.* 53:2), when it was at the lowest, but he grew up higher than the heavens. It is not with the trees of righteousness as it was with the trees of paradise, which were created all perfect at the first. The seeds of all the creatures in the present goodly frame of the world were hid in the chaos, in that confused mass at the first, out of which God commanded all creatures to arise. In the small seeds of plants lie hidden both bulk and branches, bud and fruit. In a few principles lie hidden all comfortable conclusions of holy truth. All these glorious fireworks of zeal and holiness in the saints had their beginning from a few sparks.

Let us not therefore be discouraged at the small beginnings of grace, but look on ourselves as elected to be 'holy and without blame' (*Eph.* 1:4). Let us look on our imperfect beginning only to enforce further striving to perfection, and to keep us in a low opinion of ourselves. Otherwise, in case of discouragement, we must consider ourselves as Christ does, who looks on us as those he intends to fit for himself. Christ values us by what we shall be, and by what we are elected unto. We call a little plant a tree, because it is growing up to be so. 'Who has despised the day of small things?' (*Zech.* 4:10). Christ would not have us despise little things.

The glorious angels disdain not attendance on little ones – little in their own eyes, and little in the eyes of the world. Grace, though little in quantity, yet is much in vigour and worth. It is Christ that raises the worth of little and mean places and persons. Bethlehem was the least (*Mic.* 5:2; *Matt.* 2:6), and yet not the least; the least in itself, not the least in respect that Christ was born there. The second temple (*Hag.* 2:9) came short of the outward magnificence of the former; yet it was more glorious than the first because Christ came into it. The Lord of the temple came into his own temple. The pupil of the eye is very little, yet sees a great part of the heaven at once. A pearl, though little, yet is of much esteem. Nothing in the world is of so good use as the least grain of grace.

GRACE IS MINGLED WITH CORRUPTION

But grace is not only little, but mingled with corruption; therefore a Christian is said to be smoking flax. So we see that grace does not do away with corruption all at once, but some is left for believers to fight with. The purest actions of the purest men need Christ to perfume them; and this is his office. When we pray, we need to pray again for Christ to pardon the defects of our prayers. Consider some instances of this smoking flax:

Moses at the Red Sea, being in a great perplexity, and knowing not what to say, or which way to turn, groaned to God. No doubt this was a great conflict in him. In great distresses we know not what to pray, but the Spirit makes request with sighs that cannot be expressed (*Rom.* 8:26). Broken hearts can yield but broken prayers.

When David was before the king of Gath (*1 Sam.* 21:13) and disfigured himself in an uncomely manner, in that smoke there was some fire also. You may see what an excellent psalm he makes upon that occasion, Psalm 34, in which, on the basis of experience, he says, 'The LORD is nigh unto them that are of a broken heart' (*Psa.* 34:18). 'I said in my haste, I am cut off from before thine eyes.' There is smoke. 'Nevertheless thou heardest the voice of my supplications' (*Psa.* 31:22). There is fire. 'Lord, save us: we perish' (*Matt.* 8:25), cry the disciples. Here is smoke of infidelity, yet so much light of faith as stirred them up to pray to Christ. 'Lord, I believe.' There is light.

'Help thou mine unbelief.' There is smoke (*Mark* 9:24). Jonah cries, 'I am cast out of thy sight.' There is smoke. 'Yet I will look again toward thy holy temple.' There is light (*Jon.* 2:4).

'O wretched man that I am!', says Paul, with a sense of his corruption. Yet he breaks out into thanks to God through Jesus Christ our Lord (*Rom.* 7:24).

'I sleep,' says the church in the Song of Solomon, 'but my heart waketh' (*Song of Sol.* 5:2). In the seven churches, which for their light are called 'seven golden candlesticks' (*Rev.* 2 and 3), most of them had much smoke with their light.

The reason for this mixture is that we carry about us a double principle, grace and nature. The end of it is especially to preserve us from those two dangerous rocks which our natures are prone to dash upon, security and pride, and to force us to pitch our rest on justification, not sanctification, which, besides imperfection, has some stains. Our spiritual fire is like our ordinary fire here below, that is, mixed. Fire is most pure in its own element above; so shall all our graces be when we are where we would be, in heaven, which is our proper element.

From this mixture arises the fact that the people of God have so different judgments of themselves, looking sometimes at the work of grace, sometimes at the remainder of corruption, and when they look upon that, then they think they have no grace. Though they love Christ in his ordinances and children, yet they dare not claim so near acquaintance as to be his. Even as a candle in the socket sometimes shows its light, and sometimes the show of light is lost; so sometimes they are well persuaded of themselves, sometimes at a loss.

4. Christ Will Not Quench the Smoking Flax

The second observation concerning the weak and small beginnings of grace is that Christ will not quench the smoking flax. This is so for two principal reasons. First, because this spark is from heaven: it is his own, it is kindled by his own Spirit. And secondly, it tends to the glory of his powerful grace in his children that he preserves light in the midst of darkness, a spark in the midst of the swelling waters of corruption.

THE LEAST SPARK OF GRACE IS PRECIOUS

There is an especial blessing in that little spark. 'As the new wine is found in the cluster, and one saith, Destroy it not; for a blessing is in it: so will I do for my servants' sakes' (*Isa.* 65:8). We see how our Saviour Christ bore with Thomas in his doubting (*John* 20:27), and with the two disciples that went to Emmaus, who wavered as to whether he came to redeem Israel or not (*Luke* 24:21). He quenched not that little light in Peter, which was smothered: Peter denied him, but he denied not Peter (*Luke* 22:61). 'If thou wilt, thou canst,' said one poor man in the Gospel (*Matt.* 8:2). 'If thou canst do anything,' said another (*Mark* 9:22). Both were smoking flax. Neither of them was quenched. If Christ had stood upon his own greatness, he would have rejected him that came with his 'if'. But Christ answers his 'if' with a gracious and absolute grant, 'I will, be thou clean.' The woman that was diseased with an issue did but touch, with a trembling hand, and but the hem of his garment, and yet she went away both healed and comforted. In the seven churches (*Rev.* 2 and 3), we see that Christ acknowledges and cherishes anything that was good in them. Because the disciples slept due to infirmity, being oppressed with grief, our Saviour Christ frames a comfortable excuse for them, 'The spirit indeed is willing, but the flesh is weak' (*Matt.* 26:41).

If Christ should not be merciful, he would miss of his own ends: 'There is forgiveness with thee, that thou mayest be feared' (*Psa.* 130:4). Now all are welcome to come under that banner of love which he spreads over his own: 'Unto thee shall all flesh come' (*Psa.* 65:2). He uses moderation and care, 'lest the spirit should fail before him, and the souls which he hath made' (*Isa.* 57:16). Christ's heart yearned, the text says, when he saw the people without meat, 'lest they faint in the way' (*Matt.* 15:32); much more will he have regard for the preventing of our spiritual faintings.

SUPPORT THE WEAK

Here see the opposite dispositions in the holy nature of Christ and the impure nature of man. Man for a little smoke will quench the light. Christ, we see, ever cherishes even the least beginnings. How he bore with the many imperfections of his poor disciples! If he did sharply check them, it was in love, and that they might shine the brighter. Can we have a better pattern to follow than this from him by whom we hope to be saved? 'We then that are strong ought to bear the infirmities of the weak' (*Rom.* 15:1). 'I am made all things to all men, that I might by all means save some' (*1 Cor.* 9:22). Oh, that this gaining and winning disposition were more in many! Many, so far as in us lies, are lost for want of encouragement. See how that faithful fisher of men, the Apostle Paul, labours to catch his judge: 'I know that thou believest the prophets' (*Acts* 26:27), and then wishes him all saving good, but not bonds. He might have added them too, but he would not discourage one that responded. He would therefore wish Agrippa only that which was good in religion. How careful was our blessed Saviour of little ones, that they might not be offended! How he defends his disciples from malicious imputations of the Pharisees! How careful not to put new wine into old vessels (*Matt.* 9:17), not to alienate new beginners with the austerities of religion (as some do indiscreetly). Oh, says he, they shall have time to fast when I am gone, and strength to fast when the Holy Ghost is come upon them.

It is not the best way, to assail young beginners with minor matters, but to show them a more excellent way and train them in fundamental points. Then other things will not gain credence with them. It is not amiss to conceal their defects, to excuse some failings, to commend their performances, to encourage their progress, to remove all difficulties out of their way, to help them in every way to bear the yoke of religion with greater ease, to bring them to love God and his service, lest they acquire a distaste for it before they know it. For the most part we see that Christ plants in young beginners a love which we call their 'first love' (*Rev.* 2:4), to carry them through their profession with more delight, and does not expose them to crosses before they have gathered strength; as we bring on young plants and fence them from the weather until they be rooted. Mercy to others should move us to deny ourselves in our liberties oftentimes, in case of offending weak ones. It is the 'little ones' that are offended (*Matt.* 18:6). The weakest are most ready to think themselves despised; therefore we should be most careful to give them satisfaction.

It would be a good contest amongst Christians, one to labour to give no offence, and the other to labour to take none. The best men are severe to themselves, tender over others. Yet people should not tire and wear out the patience of others: nor should the weaker so far demand moderation from others as to rely upon their indulgence and so to rest in their own infirmities, with danger to their own souls and scandal to the church.

Neither must they despise the gifts of God in others, which grace teaches to honour wheresoever they are found, but know their parts and place, and not undertake anything above their measure, which may make their persons and their case obnoxious to scorn. When blindness and boldness, ignorance and arrogance, weakness and wilfulness, meet together in men, it renders them odious to God, burdensome in society, dangerous in their counsels, disturbers of better purposes, intractable and incapable of better direction, miserable in the issue. Where Christ shows his gracious power in weakness, he does it by letting men understand themselves so far as to breed humility, and magnify God's love to such as they are. He does it as a preservative against discouragements from weakness, to bring men into a less distance from grace, as an advantage to poverty of spirit, rather than greatness of condition and parts, which yield to corrupt nature fuel for pride. Christ refuses none for weakness of parts, that none should be discouraged, but accepts none for greatness, that none should be lifted up with that which is of so little reckoning with God. It is no great matter how dull the scholar be when Christ takes upon him to be the teacher, who, as he prescribes what to understand, so he gives understanding itself, even to the simplest.

The church suffers much from weak ones, therefore we may assert our liberty to deal with them, though mildly, yet oftentimes directly. The scope of true love is to make the party better, which concealment oftentimes hinders. With some a spirit of meekness prevails most, but with some a rod. Some must be 'pulled out of the fire' (*Jude* 23) with violence, and they will bless God for us in the day of their visitation. We see that our Saviour multiplies woe upon woe when he has to deal with hard-hearted hypocrites (*Matt.* 23:13), for hypocrites need stronger conviction than gross sinners, because their will is bad, and therefore usually their conversion is violent. A hard knot must have an answerable wedge, else, in a cruel pity, we betray their souls. A sharp reproof sometimes is a precious pearl and a sweet balm. The wounds of secure sinners will not be healed with sweet words. The Holy Ghost came as well in fiery tongues as in the likeness of a dove, and the same Holy Spirit will vouchsafe a spirit of prudence and discretion, which is the salt to season all our words and actions. And such wisdom will teach us 'to speak a word in season' (*Isa.* 50:4), both to the weary, and likewise to the secure soul. And, indeed, he has need of 'the tongue of the learned' that shall either raise up or cast down, though in this place I speak of mildness towards those that are weak and are sensible of it. These we must bring on gently, and drive softly, as Jacob did his cattle (*Gen.* 33:14), according to their pace, and as his children were able to endure.

Weak Christians are like glasses which are hurt with the least violent usage, but if gently handled will continue a long time. This honour of gentle use we are to give to the weaker vessels (*1 Pet.* 3:7), by which we shall both preserve them and likewise make them useful to the church and ourselves.

In diseased bodies, if all ill humours be purged out, you shall purge life and all away. Therefore, though God says that he will 'refine them as silver is refined' (*Zech.* 13:9), yet he said he had 'refined thee, but not with silver' (*Isa.* 48:10), that is, not so exactly as that no dross remains, for he has respect to our weakness. Perfect refining is for another world, for the world of the souls of perfect men.

5. *The Spirit of Mercy Should Move Us*

Preachers need to take heed therefore how they deal with young believers. Let them be careful not to pitch matters too high, making things necessary evidences of grace which agree not to the experience of many a good Christian, and laying salvation and damnation upon things that are not fit to bear so great a weight. In this way men are needlessly cast down and may not soon be raised up again by themselves or others. The ambassadors of so gentle a Saviour should not be overbearing, setting up themselves in the hearts of people where Christ alone should sit as in his own temple. Too much respect to man was one of the inlets of popery. 'Let a man so account of us, as of the ministers of Christ' (*1 Cor.* 4:1), neither more nor less, just so much. How careful was Paul in cases of conscience not to lay a snare upon any weak conscience.

SIMPLICITY AND HUMILITY

Preachers should take heed likewise that they hide not their meaning in dark speeches, speaking in the clouds. Truth fears nothing so much as concealment, and desires nothing so much as clearly to be laid open to the view of all. When it is most unadorned, it is most lovely and powerful. Our blessed Saviour, as he took our nature upon him, so he took upon him our familiar manner of speech, which was part of his voluntary abasement. Paul was a profound man, yet he became as a nurse to the weaker sort (*1 Thess.* 2:7).

That spirit of mercy that was in Christ should move his servants to be content to abase themselves for the good of the meanest. What made the kingdom of heaven 'suffer violence' (*Matt.* 11:12) after John the Baptist's time, but that comfortable truths were laid open with such plainness and evidence that the people were so affected with them as to offer a holy violence to obtain them?

Christ chose those to preach mercy who had felt most mercy, as Peter and Paul, that they might be examples of what they taught. Paul became all things to all men (*1 Cor.* 9:22), stooping unto them for their good. Christ came down from heaven and emptied himself of majesty in tender love to souls. Shall we not come down from our high conceits to do any poor soul good? Shall man be proud after God has been humble? We see the ministers of Satan turn themselves into all shapes to 'make one proselyte' (*Matt.* 23:15). We see ambitious men study accommodation of themselves to the humours of those by whom they hope to be raised, and shall not we study application of ourselves to Christ, by whom we hope to be advanced, nay, are already sitting with him in heavenly places? After we are gained to Christ ourselves, we should labour to gain others to Christ. Holy ambition and covetousness will move us to put upon ourselves the disposition of Christ. But we must put off ourselves first.

Again we should not rack their wits with curious or 'doubtful disputations' (*Rom.* 14:1), for so we shall distract and tire them, and give occasion to make them cast off the care of all. That age of the church which was most fertile in subtle questions was most barren in religion; for it makes people think religion to be only a matter of cleverness, in tying and untying of knots. The brains of men inclining that way are hotter usually than their hearts.

Yet notwithstanding, when we are cast into times and places wherein doubts are raised about principal points, here people ought to labour to be established. God suffers questions oftentimes to arise for trial of our love and exercise of our abilities. Nothing is so certain as that which is certain after doubts. Shaking settles and roots. In a contentious age, it is a wise thing to be a Christian, and to know what to pitch our souls upon. It is an office of love here to take away the stones, and to smooth the way to heaven. Therefore, we must take heed that, under pretence of avoidance of disputes, we do not suffer an adverse party to get ground upon the truth; for thus may we easily betray both the truth of God and souls of men.

And likewise those are failing that, by overmuch austerity, drive back troubled souls from having comfort by them, for, as a result of this, many smother their temptations, and burn inwardly, because they have none into whose bosom they may vent their grief and ease their souls.

We must neither bind where God looses, nor loose where God binds, neither open where God shuts, nor shut where God opens. The right use of the keys is always successful. In personal application, there must be great heed taken; for a man may be a false prophet, and yet speak the truth. If it be not a truth to the person to whom he speaks, if he grieve those whom God has not grieved by unseasonable truths, or by comforts in an ill way, the hearts of the wicked may be strengthened. One man's meat may be another's poison.

If we look to the general temper of these times, rousing and waking Scriptures are fittest; yet there are many broken spirits who need soft and comforting words. Even in the worst time the prophets mingled sweet comfort for the hidden remnant of faithful people. God has comfort. The prophet is told, 'Comfort ye my people' (*Isa.* 40:1), as well as, 'Lift up thy voice as a trumpet' (*Isa.* 58:1).

SOUND JUDGMENT

And here likewise there needs a caveat. Mercy does not rob us of our right judgment, so as to take stinking fire-brands for smoking flax. None will claim mercy more of others than those who deserve due severity. This example does not countenance lukewarmness, nor too much indulgence to those that need quickening. Cold diseases must have hot remedies. It made for the just commendation of the church of Ephesus that it could not bear them which were evil (*Rev.* 2:2). We should so bear with others as to manifest also a dislike of evil. Our Saviour Christ would not forbear sharp reproof where he saw dangerous infirmities in his most beloved disciples. It brings under a curse to do the work of the Lord deceitfully (*Jer.* 48:10), even where it is a work of just severity, as when it is sheathing the sword in the bowels of the enemy. And those whom we suffer to be betrayed by their worst enemies, their sins, will have just cause to curse us one day.

It is hard to preserve just bounds of mercy and severity without a spirit above our own, by which we ought to desire to be led in all things. That wisdom which dwells with prudence (*Prov.* 8:12) will guide us in these particulars, without which virtue is not virtue, truth not truth. The rule and the case must be laid together; for if there be not a keen insight, seeming likeness in conditions will give rise to errors in our opinions of them. Those fiery, tempestuous and destructive spirits in popery that seek to promote their religion by cruelty show that they are strangers to that wisdom which is from above, which makes men gentle, peaceable and ready to show that mercy which they themselves have felt. It is a way of prevailing agreeable both to Christ and to man's nature to prevail by some forbearance and moderation.

And yet often we see a false spirit in those that call for moderation. Their doing so is but to carry their own projects with the greater strength; and if they prevail they will hardly show that moderation to others which they now call for from others. And there is a proud kind of moderation likewise, when men will take upon them to censure both parties, as if they were wiser than both, although, if the spirit be right, an onlooker may see more than those that are in conflict.

HOW THOSE IN AUTHORITY SHOULD ACT

In the censures of the church, it is more suitable to the spirit of Christ to incline to the milder part, and not to kill a fly on the forehead with a mallet, nor shut men out of heaven for a trifle. The very snuffers (wick-trimmers) of the tabernacle were made of pure gold, to shew the purity of those censures whereby the light of the church is kept bright. The power that is given to the church is given for edification, not destruction. How careful was Paul that the incestuous Corinthian (*2 Cor.* 2:7), if he repented, should not be swallowed up with too much grief. Civil magistrates, for civil exigencies and reasons of state, must let the law have its course; yet thus far they should imitate this mild king, as not to mingle bitterness and passion with authority derived from God. Authority is a beam of God's majesty, and prevails most where there is least mixture of that which is man's. It requires more than ordinary wisdom to manage it aright. This string must not be too tight, nor too loose. Justice is a harmonious thing. Herbs hot or cold beyond a certain degree, kill. We see even contrary elements preserved in one body by wisely tempering them together. Justice in rigour is often extreme injustice, where some considerable circumstances should incline to moderation; and the reckoning will be easier for bending rather to moderation than rigour.

Insolent behaviour toward miserable persons, if humbled, is unseemly in any who look for mercy themselves. Misery should be a lodestone of mercy, not a footstool for pride to trample on. Sometimes it falls out that those who are under the government of others are most injurious by waywardness and harsh censures, herein disparaging and discouraging the endeavours of superiors for public good. In so great weakness of man's nature, and especially in this crazy age of the world, we ought to take in good part any moderate happiness we enjoy by government, and not be altogether as a nail in the wound, exasperating things by misconstruction. Here love should have a mantle to cast upon lesser errors of those above us. Oftentimes the poor man is the oppressor by unjust clamours. We should labour to give the best interpretation to the actions of governors that the nature of the actions will possibly bear.

WE ARE DEBTORS TO THE WEAK

In the last place, there is something for private Christians, even for all of us in our common relations, to take notice of: we are debtors to the weak in many things.

1. Let us be watchful in the use of our liberty, and labour to be inoffensive in our behaviour, that our

example compel them not. There is a commanding force in an example, as there was in Peter (*Gal.* 2). Looseness of life is cruelty to ourselves and to the souls of others. Though we cannot keep those who will perish from perishing, yet if we do that which is apt of itself to destroy the souls of others their ruin is imputable to us.

2.   Let men take heed of taking up Satan's office, in misrepresenting the good actions of others, as he did Job's case, 'Doth Job fear God for nought?' (*Job* 1:9), or slandering their persons, judging of them according to the wickedness that is in their own hearts. The devil gets more by such discouragements and reproaches that are cast upon religion than by fire and faggot. These, as unseasonable frosts, nip all gracious inclinations in the bud, and as much as in them lies, with Herod, labour to kill Christ in young professors. A Christian is a hallowed and a sacred thing, Christ's temple; and he that destroys his temple, him will Christ destroy (*1 Cor.*3:17).

3.   Among the things that are to be taken heed of, there is among ordinary Christians a bold usurpation of censure towards others, not considering their tempt-ations. Some will unchurch and unbrother in a passion. But ill humours do not alter true relations; though the child in a fit should disclaim the mother, yet the mother will not disclaim the child.

There is therefore in these judging times good ground of James's caveat that there should not be 'many masters' (*James* 3:1), that we should not smite one another by hasty censures, especially in things of an indifferent nature; some things are as the mind of him is that does them, or does them not; for both may be unto the Lord.

A holy aim in things neither clearly right nor wrong makes the judgments of men, although seemingly contrary, yet not so much blameable. Christ, for the good aims he sees in us, overlooks any ill in them, so far as not to lay it to our charge. Men must not be too curious in prying into the weaknesses of others. We should labour rather to see what they have that is for eternity, to incline our heart to love them, than into that weakness which the Spirit of God will in time consume, to estrange us. Some think it strength of grace to endure nothing in the weaker, whereas the strongest are readiest to bear with the infirmities of the weak.

Where most holiness is, there is most moderation, where it may be without prejudice of piety to God and the good of others. We see in Christ a marvellous temper of absolute holiness, with great moderation. What would have become of our salvation, if he had stood upon terms, and not stooped thus low unto us? We need not affect to be more holy than Christ. It is no flattery to do as he does, so long as it is to edification.

The Holy Ghost is content to dwell in smoky, offensive souls. Oh, that that Spirit would breathe into our spirits the same merciful disposition! We endure the bitterness of wormwood, and other distasteful plants and herbs, only because we have some experience of some wholesome quality in them; and why should we reject men of useful parts and graces, only for some harshness of disposition, which, as it is offensive to us, so it grieves themselves?

Grace, while we live here, is in souls which, because they are imperfectly renewed, dwell in bodies subject to several humours, and these will incline the soul sometimes to excess in one passion, sometimes to excess in another. Bucer was a deep and a moderate divine. After long experience he resolved to refuse none in whom he saw *aliquid Christi,* something of Christ. The best Christians in this state of imperfection are like gold that is a little too light, which needs some grains of allowance to make it pass. You must grant the best their allowance.

We must supply out of our love and mercy that which we see wanting in them. The church of Christ is a common hospital, wherein all are in some measure sick of some spiritual disease or other, so all have occasion to exercise the spirit of wisdom and meekness.

So that we may do this the better, let us put upon ourselves the Spirit of Christ. There is a majesty in the Spirit of God. Corruption will hardly yield to corruption in another. Pride is intolerable to pride. The weapons of this warfare must not be carnal (*2 Cor.* 10:4). The great apostles would not set upon the work of the ministry until they were 'endued with power from on high' (*Luke* 24:49). The Spirit will only work with his own tools. And we should think what affection Christ would carry to the party in this case. That great physician, as he had a quick eye and a healing tongue, so had he a gentle hand, and a tender heart.

And, further, let us take to ourselves the condition of him with whom we deal. We are, or have been, or may be in that condition ourselves. Let us make the case our own, and also consider in what near relation a Christian stands to us, even as a brother, a fellow-member, heir of the same salvation. And therefore let us take upon ourselves a tender care of them in every way; and especially in cherishing the peace of their consciences. Conscience is a tender and delicate thing, and must be so treated. It is like a lock: if its workings are faulty, it will be troublesome to open.

6. *Marks of the Smoking Flax*

To determine whether we are this smoking flax which Christ will not quench, we must remember these rules:

We must have two eyes, one to see imperfections in ourselves and others, the other to see what is good. 'I am black,' says the church, 'but comely' (*Song of Sol.* 1:5). Those who are given to quarrelling with themselves always lack comfort, and through their infirmities they are prone to feed on such bitter things as will most nourish that disease which troubles them. These delight to be looking on the dark side of the cloud only.

We must not judge of ourselves always according to present feeling, for in temptations we shall see nothing but smoke of distrustful thoughts. Fire may be raked up in the ashes, though not seen. Life in the winter is hid in the root.

We must beware of false reasoning, such as: because our fire does not blaze out as others, therefore we have no fire at all. By false conclusions we may come to sin against the commandment in bearing false witness against ourselves. The prodigal would not say he was no son, but that he was not worthy to be called a son (*Luke* 15:19). We must neither trust to false evidence, nor deny true; for so we should dishonour the work of God's Spirit in us, and lose the help of that evidence which would cherish our love to Christ, and arm us against Satan's discouragements. Some are as faulty in this way as if they had been hired by Satan, the 'accuser of the brethren' (*Rev.* 12:10), to plead for him in accusing themselves.

OUR RULE IS THE COVENANT OF GRACE

We must acknowledge that in the covenant of grace God requires the truth of grace, not any certain measure; and a spark of fire is fire, as well as the whole element. Therefore we must look to grace in the spark as well as in the flame. All have not the like *strong,* though they have the like *precious,* faith (*2 Pet.* 1:1), whereby they lay hold of, and put on, the perfect righteousness of Christ. A weak hand may receive a rich jewel. A few grapes will show that the plant is a vine, and not a thorn. It is one thing to be deficient in grace, and another thing to lack grace altogether. God knows we have nothing of ourselves, therefore in the covenant of grace he requires no more than he gives, but gives what he requires, and accepts what he gives: 'If she be not able to bring a lamb, then she shall bring two turtle doves' (*Lev.* 12:8). What is the gospel itself but a merciful moderation, in which Christ's obedience is esteemed ours, and our sins laid upon him, wherein God, from being a judge, becomes our Father, pardoning our sins and accepting our obedience, though feeble and blemished? We are now brought to heaven under the covenant of grace by a way of love and mercy.

It will prove a special help to know distinctly the difference between the covenant of works and the covenant of grace, between Moses and Christ. Moses, without any mercy, breaks all bruised reeds, and quenches all smoking flax. For the law requires personal, perpetual and perfect obedience from the heart, and that under a most terrible curse, but gives no strength. It is a severe task-master, like Pharaoh's, requiring the whole tale of bricks and yet giving no straw. Christ comes with blessing after blessing, even upon those whom Moses had cursed, and with healing balm for those wounds which Moses had made.

The same duties are required in both covenants, such as to love the Lord with all our hearts and with all our souls (*Deut.* 6:5). In the covenant of works, this must be fulfilled absolutely, but under the covenant of grace it must have an evangelical mitigation. A sincere endeavour proportionable to grace received is accepted (and so it must be understood of Josiah, and others, when it is said they did that which was right in the sight of the Lord).

The law is sweetened by the gospel, and becomes delightful to the inner man (*Rom.* 7:22). Under this gracious covenant, sincerity is perfection. This is the death in the pot of the Roman religion, that they confound the two covenants, and it deadens the comfort of drooping ones that they cannot distinguish them. And thus they suffer themselves to be held under bondage when Christ has set them free, and stay in the prison when Christ has set open the doors before them.

We must remember that grace sometimes is so little as to be indiscernible to us. The Spirit sometimes has secret operations in us which we know not for the present, but Christ knows. Sometimes, in bitterness of temptation, when the spirit struggles with a sense of God's anger, we are apt to think God an enemy. A troubled soul is like troubled water: we can see nothing in it, and, so far as it is not cleansed, it will cast up mire and dirt. It is full of objections against itself, yet for the most part we may discern something of the hidden life, and of these smothered sparks. In a gloomy day there is so much light that we may know it to be day and not night; so there is something in a Christian under a cloud whereby he may be discerned to be a true believer and not a hypocrite. There is no mere darkness in the state of grace, but some beam of light whereby the kingdom of darkness does not wholly prevail.

THE PRESENCE OF THE HEAVENLY FIRE

Applying these rules, we may say:

First, *if there be any holy fire in us, it is kindled from heaven* by the Father of lights, who 'commanded the light to shine out of darkness' (*2 Cor.* 4: 6). As it is kindled by the use of means, so it is fed. The light in us and the light in the Word spring the one from the other and both from the one Holy Spirit. Therefore, in the case of those that regard not the Word, it is 'because there is no light in them' (*Isa.* 8:20). Heavenly truths must have a heavenly light to discern them. Natural men see heavenly things, not in their own proper light, but by an inferior light. In every converted man, God puts a light into the eye of his soul proportionable to the light of truths revealed to him. A carnal eye will never see spiritual things.

Secondly, *the least divine light has heat with it in some measure.* Light in the understanding produces heat of love in the affections. In the measure that the sanctified understanding sees a thing to be true or good, in that measure the will embraces it. Weak light produces weak inclinations, strong light, strong inclinations. A little spiritual light is of strength enough to answer strong objections of flesh and blood, and to see beyond all earthly allurements and opposing hindrances, presenting them as far inferior to those heavenly objects it beholds. All light that is not spiritual, because it lacks the strength of sanctifying grace, yields to every little temptation, especially when it is fitted and suited to personal inclinations. This is the reason why Christians that have light that is little for quantity, but heavenly for quality, persevere, when men of larger apprehensions sink. This prevailing of light in the soul is because, together with the spirit of illumination, there goes, in the godly, a spirit of power (*2 Tim.* 1:7) to subdue the heart to truth revealed, and to put a taste and relish into the will, suitable to the sweetness of the truth; otherwise a will that is merely natural will rise against supernatural truths, as having an antipathy and enmity against them. In the godly, holy truths are conveyed by way of a taste; gracious men have a spiritual palate as well as a spiritual eye. Grace alters the spiritual taste.

Thirdly, *where this heavenly light is kindled, it directs in the right way.* For it is given for that use, to show us the best way, and to guide us in the particular passages of life; otherwise, it is but common light, given only for the good of others. Some have light of knowledge, yet follow not that light, but are guided by carnal reason and policy, such as those the prophet speaks of, 'All ye that kindle a fire . . . walk in the light of your fire, and in the sparks that ye have kindled. This shall ye have of mine hand; ye shall lie down in sorrow' (*Isa.* 50:11). God delights to confound carnal wisdom, as enmity to him, and robbing him of his prerogative, who is God only wise. We must, therefore, walk by his light, not the blaze of our own fire. God must light our candle (*Psa.* 18:28) or else we will abide in darkness. Those sparks that are not kindled from heaven are not strong enough to keep us from lying in sorrow, though they make a greater blaze and show than the light from above, as madmen do greater things than sober men, but by a false strength: so the excess of these men's joy arises from a false light. 'The light of the wicked shall be put out' (*Job* 18:5).

The light which some men have is like lightning which, after a sudden flash, leaves them more in darkness. They can love the light as it shines, but hate it as it discovers and directs. A little holy light will enable us to keep Christ's Word, and not betray religion nor deny his name, as Christ speaks of the church of Philadelphia (*Rev.* 3:8).

Fourthly, w*here this fire is, it will sever things of diverse natures, and show a difference between such things as gold and dross.* It will sever between flesh and spirit, and show that this is of nature, this of grace. All is not ill in a bad action, or good in a good action. There is gold in ore, which God and his Spirit in us can distinguish. A carnal man's heart is like a dungeon, wherein nothing is to be seen but horror and confusion. This light makes us judicious and humble, upon clearer sight of God's purity and our own uncleanness, and makes us able to discern the work of the Spirit in another.

Fifthly, *so far as a man is spiritual, so far is light delightful to him.* He is willing to see anything amiss that he may reform, and any further service discovered that he may perform, because he truly hates ill and loves good. If he goes against light discovered, he will soon be reclaimed, because light has a friendly party within him. Therefore, at a little sight of his error, he is soon open to counsel, as David was in his intention to kill Nabal; and he blessed God afterwards, when he was stopped in an ill way (*1 Sam.* 25:32).

In the case of a carnal man, the light breaks in on him, but he labours to block its entrance. He has no delight in coming to the light. It is impossible, before the Spirit of grace has subdued the heart, that it should not sin against the light, either by resisting it, or keeping it prisoner under base lusts and burying it, as it were, in the earth, or perverting it, and so making it an agent and factor for the flesh, in searching out arguments to plead for it, or abusing that little measure of light men have, so as to keep out a greater, higher, and more heavenly light. So, at length, they make the light they have a misleading guide to utter darkness. And the reason is because the light has no friend within. The soul is in a contrary frame, and light always hinders that sinful peace that men are willing to promise themselves. Hence we see that light often enrages men more, as the sun in spring-time brings on feverish illnesses when it stirs up bodily humours rather than overcoming them.

There is nothing in the world more uneasy than the heart of a wicked man made to listen to spiritual instruction, until, like a thief, he puts out the candle so that he may sin with less restraint. Spiritual light is distinct. It apprehends spiritual good and applies it to ourselves; but common light is confused, and lets sin lie quiet. Where fire is, in any degree, it will fight everything contrary to it. God put irreconcilable hatred between light and darkness from the first; so also between good and ill, flesh and Spirit (*Gal.* 5:17). Grace will never join with sin, any more than fire with water. Fire will mingle with nothing contrary, but preserves its own purity, and is never corrupted as other elements are. Therefore, those that plead and plot for liberties for the flesh show themselves strangers from the life of God. Feeling this strife, gracious men often complain that they have no grace. But they contradict themselves in their complaints, as if a man that sees should complain he cannot see, or complain that he is asleep; whereas the very complaint, springing from a displeasure against sin, shows that there is something in him opposite to sin. Can a dead man complain? Some things, though bad in themselves, yet reveal good, as smoke reveals the presence of fire. A violent reaction in the body shows bodily vigour. Some infirmities show more good than some seemingly beautiful actions. Excess of passion in opposing evil, though not to be justified, yet shows a better spirit than a calm temper where there is just cause of being moved. It is better that the water should run somewhat muddily than not run at all. Job had more grace in his ill temper than his friends in their seemingly wise demeanour. Actions stained with some defects are more acceptable than empty compliments.

Sixthly, *fire, where it is present, is in some degree active.* So the least measure of grace *works,* as springing from the Spirit of God, who, from his operations, is compared to fire. Even in sins, when there seems nothing active but corruption, there is a contrary principle, which breaks the force of sin, so that it is not boundlessly sinful, as in those that are carnal (*Rom.* 7:13).

Seventhly, *fire makes metals pliable and malleable.* So grace, where it is given, makes the heart pliable and ready to receive all good impressions. Obstinate spirits show that they are not so much as smoking flax.

Eighthly, *fire, as much as it can, sets everything on fire.* So grace labours to produce a gracious impression in others, and make as many good as it can. Grace also makes a gracious use even of natural and civil things, and spiritualizes them. What another man does only in a civil way a gracious man will do holily. Whether he eats or drinks or whatsoever he does, he does all to the glory of God (*1 Cor.* 10:31), making everything serviceable to that ultimate end.

Ninthly, *sparks by nature fly upwards.* So the Spirit of grace carries the soul heaven-ward and sets before us holy and heavenly aims. As it was kindled from heaven, so it carries us back to heaven. The part follows the whole: fire mounts upward, so every spark to its own element. Where the aim and bent of the soul is towards God, there is grace, though opposed. The least measure of it is seen in holy desires, springing from faith and love, for we cannot desire anything which we do not believe first to be, and the desire of it issues from love. Hence desires are counted a part of the thing desired, in some measure. But these desires must be (1) *constant,* for constancy shows that they are supernaturally natural, and not enforced; (2) *directed to spiritual things,* such as to believe, to love God, not because of a particular emergency, in that one thinks one might escape some danger if one had grace, but as a loving heart is carried to the thing loved for the sake of some excellency in it; (3) *accompanied with grief when the desire is hindered,* so as to stir us up to pray: 'Oh that my ways were directed that I might keep thy statutes!' (*Psa.* 119:5); 'O wretched man that I am! Who shall deliver me?' (*Rom.* 7:24); and (4) *such desires as drive us onward still:* 'Oh, that I might serve God with more liberty. Oh, that I were more free from these offensive, unsavoury, hateful lusts!'

Tenthly, *fire, if it has any matter to feed on, enlarges itself and mounts higher and higher, and, the higher it rises, the purer is the flame.* So where true grace is, it grows in measure and purity. Smoking flax will grow to a flame; and, as it increases, so it discards what is contrary to itself and refines itself more and more. *Ignis, quo magis lucet, eo minus fumat* (As fire gives more light, it gives less smoke). Therefore, it argues a false heart to set ourselves a low standard in grace and to rest in beginnings, alleging that Christ will not quench the smoking flax. This merciful disposition in Christ is joined with perfect holiness, shown in perfect hatred to sin; for, rather than that sin should not have its deserved punishment, he became a sacrifice for sin. In this his Father's holiness and his own shone most of all. And besides this, in the work of sanctification, though he favours his work in us, yet he does not favour sin in us; for he will never take his hand from his work, until he has taken away sin, even in its very being, from our natures. The same Spirit that purified his holy human nature cleanses us by degrees to be suitable to so holy a Head, and frames the judgment and affections of all to whom he shows mercy to concur with his own, in labouring to further his end of abolishing sin out of our natures.

7. *Help for the Weak*

By meditation on these rules and signs, much comfort may be brought to the souls of the weakest. That it may be in greater abundance, let me add something to help them over some few ordinary objections and secret thoughts against themselves which, getting within the heart, oftentimes keep them low.

TEMPTATIONS WHICH HINDER COMFORT

1. Some think they have no faith at all because they have no full assurance, whereas the fairest fire that can be will have some smoke. The best actions will smell of the smoke. The mortar wherein garlic has been stamped will always smell of it; so all our actions will savour something of the old man.

2. In weakness of body some think grace dies, because their performances are feeble, their spirits, which are the instruments of their souls' actions, being weakened. But they do not consider that God regards the hidden sighs of those that lack abilities to express them outwardly. He that pronounces those blessed that consider the poor will have a merciful consideration of such himself.

3. Some again are haunted with hideous representations to their imaginations, and with vile and unworthy thoughts of God, of Christ, of the Word, which, as busy flies, disquiet and molest their peace. These are cast in like wildfire by Satan, as may be discerned by the strangeness, the strength and violence, and the horribleness of them even to corrupt nature. A pious soul is no more guilty of them than Benjamin was when Joseph's cup was put into his sack. Among other helps recommended by godly writers, such as detestation of them and diversion from them to other things, let this be one, to complain to Christ against them, and to fly under the wings of his protection, and to desire him to take our part against his and our enemy. Shall every sin and blasphemy of man be forgiven, and not these blasphemous thoughts, which have the devil for their father, when Christ himself was molested in this way so that he might succour all poor souls in this condition?

But there is a difference between Christ and us in this case. Because Satan had nothing of his own in Christ his suggestions left no impression at all in his holy nature, but, as sparks falling into the sea, were presently quenched. Satan's temptations of Christ were only suggestions on Satan's part, and apprehensions of the vileness of them on Christ's part. To apprehend ill suggested by another is not ill. It was Christ's grievance, but Satan's sin. But thus he yielded himself to be tempted, that he might both pity us in our conflicts, and train us up to manage our spiritual weapons as he did. Christ could have overcome him by power, but he did it by argument. But when Satan comes to us, he finds something of his own in us, which holds correspondence and has intelligence with him. There is the same enmity in our nature to God and goodness, in some degree, that is in Satan himself. Therefore his temptations fasten, for the most part, some taint upon us. And if there were no devil to suggest, yet sinful thoughts would arise from within us, though none were cast in from without. We have a mint of them within. These thoughts, if the soul dwell on them so long as to suck or draw from and by them any sinful delight, then they leave a more heavy guilt upon the soul, hinder our sweet communion with God, interrupt our peace, and put a contrary relish into the soul, disposing it to greater sins. All scandalous actions are only thoughts at the first. Ill thoughts are as little thieves, which, creeping in at the window, open the door to greater. Thoughts are seeds of actions. These, especially when they are helped forward by Satan, make the life of many good Christians almost a martyrdom. In this case it is an unsound comfort that some minister, that ill thoughts arise from nature, and what is natural is excusable. We must know that nature, as it came out of God's hands in the beginning, had no such risings out of it. The soul, as inspired of God, had no such unsavoury breathings. But since it betrayed itself by sin it is, in some sort, natural to it to forge sinful imaginations, and to be a furnace of such sparks. And this is an aggravation of the sinfulness of natural corruption, that it is so deeply rooted and so generally spread in our nature.

It promotes humiliation to know the whole breadth and depth of sin. But the fact that our nature now, so far as it is unrenewed, is so unhappily fruitful in ill thoughts, ministers this comfort, that it is not our case alone, as if our condition in this were different from others, as some have been tempted to think, even almost to despair. None, say they, have such a loathsome nature as I have. This springs from ignorance of the spreading of original sin, for what can come from an unclean thing but that which is unclean? 'As in water face answereth to face, so the [polluted] heart of man to man' (*Prov.* 27:19), where grace has not made some difference. As in annoyances from Satan, so here, the best way is to lay open our complaints to Christ, and cry with Paul, 'O wretched man that I am! who shall deliver me from the body of this death?' (*Rom.* 7:24). On giving vent to his distress, he presently found comfort, for he breaks into thanksgiving, 'I thank God.' And it is good to profit from this, to hate this offensive body of death more, and to draw nearer to God, as that holy man did after his 'foolish' and 'beastly' thoughts (*Psa.* 73:22 and 28), and so to keep our hearts closer to God, seasoning them with heavenly meditations in the morning, storing up good matter, so that our heart may be a good treasury, while we beg of Christ his Holy Spirit to stop that cursed issue and to be a living spring of better thoughts in us. Nothing more abases the spirits of holy men that desire to delight in God after they have escaped the common defilements of the world than these unclean issues of spirit, as being most contrary to God, who is a pure Spirit. But the very irksomeness of them yields matter of comfort against them. They force the soul to all spiritual exercises, to watchfulness and a more near walking with God, and to raise itself to thoughts of a higher nature, such as those which the truth of God, the works of God, the communion of saints, the mystery of godliness, the terror of the Lord, and the excellency of the state of a Christian and a conversation suitable to it, do abundantly minister. They discover to us a necessity of daily purging and pardoning grace, and of seeking to be found in Christ, and so bring the best often upon their knees.

Our chief comfort is that our blessed Saviour, as he bade Satan depart from him, after he had given way awhile to his insolence (*Matt.* 4:10), so he will command him to be gone from us, when it shall be good for us. He must be gone at a word. And Christ can and will likewise, in his own time, rebuke the rebellious and extravagant stirrings of our hearts and bring all the thoughts of the inner man into subjection to himself.

4. Some think, when they become more troubled with the smoke of corruption than they were before, therefore they are worse than they were. It is true that corruptions appear now more than before, but they are less.

For, first, the more sin is seen, the more it is hated, and therefore it is less. Dust particles are in a room before the sun shines, but they only appear then.

Secondly, the nearer contraries are one to another, the sharper is the conflict between them. Now, of all enemies the spirit and the flesh are nearest one to another, being both in the soul of a regenerate man, in the faculties of the soul, and in every action that springs from those faculties, and therefore it is no marvel that the soul, the seat of this battle, thus divided within itself, is as smoking flax.

Thirdly, the more grace, the more spiritual life, and the more spiritual life, the more antipathy to the contrary. Therefore none are so aware of corruption as those whose souls are most alive.

Fourthly, when men give themselves up to self-indulgence, their corruptions do not trouble them, as not being bound and tied up; but when once grace suppresses their extravagant and licentious excesses, then the flesh boils, as disdaining to be confined. Yet they are better now than they were before. That matter which yields smoke was in the torch before it was lighted, but it is not offensive till the torch begins to burn. Let such know that if the smoke be once offensive to them, it is a sign that there is light. It is better to enjoy the benefit of light, though with smoke, than to be altogether in the dark.

Nor is smoke so offensive to us as light is pleasant to us, since it yields an evidence of the truth of grace in the heart. Therefore, though it is cumbersome in the conflict, yet it is comfortable as evidence. It is better that corruption should offend us now than, by giving way to it to gain a little peace, to lose comfort afterwards. Let such therefore as are at variance and odds with their corruptions look on this text as their portion of comfort.

WEAKNESS SHOULD NOT KEEP US FROM DUTY

It should encourage us to duty that Christ will not quench the smoking flax, but blow on it till it flames. Some are loath to do good because they feel their hearts rebelling, and duties turn out badly. We should not avoid good actions because of the infirmities attending them. Christ looks more at the good in them which he means to cherish than the ill in them which he means to abolish. Though eating increases a disease, a sick man will still eat, so that nature may gain strength against the disease. So, though sin cleaves to what we do, yet let us do it, since we have to deal with so good a Lord, and the more strife we meet with, the more acceptance we shall have. Christ loves to taste of the good fruits that come from us, even though they will always savour of our old nature.

A Christian complains he cannot pray. 'Oh, I am troubled with so many distracting thoughts, and never more than now!' But has he put into your heart a desire to pray? Then he will hear the desires of his own Spirit in you. 'We know not what we should pray for as we ought' (nor how to do anything else as we ought), but the Spirit helps our infirmities with 'groanings which cannot be uttered' (*Rom.* 8:26), which are not hid from God. 'My groaning is not hid from thee' (*Psa.* 38:9). God can pick sense out of a confused prayer. These desires cry louder in his ears than your sins. Sometimes a Christian has such confused thoughts that he can say nothing but, as a child, cries, 'O Father', not able to express what he needs, like Moses at the Red Sea. These stirrings of spirit touch the heart of God and melt him into compassion towards us, when they come from the Spirit of adoption, and from a striving to be better.

'Oh, but is it possible', thinks the misgiving heart, 'that so holy a God should accept such a prayer?' Yes, he will accept that which is his own, and pardon that which is ours. Jonah prayed in the fish's belly (*Jon.* 2:1), being burdened with the guilt of sin, yet God heard him. Let not, therefore, infirmities discourage us. James takes away this objection (*James* 5:17). Some might object, 'If I were as holy as Elijah, then my prayers might be regarded.' 'But,' says he, 'Elijah was a man subject to like passions as we are.' He had his passions as well as we, or do we think that God heard him because he was without fault? Surely not. But look at the promises: 'Call upon me in the day of trouble: I will deliver thee' (*Psa.* 50:15). 'Ask, and it shall be given you' (*Matt.* 7:7) and others like these. God accepts our prayers, though weak, because we are his own children, and they come from his own Spirit; because they are according to his own will; and because they are offered in Christ's mediation, and he takes them, and mingles them with his own incense (*Rev.* 8:3).

There is never a holy sigh, never a tear we shed, which is lost. And as every grace increases by exercise of itself, so does the grace of prayer. By prayer we learn to pray. So, likewise, we should take heed of a spirit of discouragement in all other holy duties, since we have so gracious a Saviour. Pray as we are able, hear as we are able, strive as we are able, do as we are able, according to the measure of grace received. God in Christ will cast a gracious eye upon that which is his own.

Would Paul do nothing because he could not do the good that he would? No, he 'pressed toward the mark'.

Let us not be cruel to ourselves when Christ is thus gracious. There is a certain meekness of spirit whereby we yield thanks to God for any ability at all, and rest quiet with the measure of grace received, seeing it is God's good pleasure it should be so, who gives the will and the deed, yet not so as to rest from further endeavours. But when, with faithful endeavour, we come short of what we would be, and short of what others are, then know for our comfort, Christ will not quench the smoking flax, and that sincerity and truth, as we said before, with endeavour of growth, is our perfection.

What God says of Jeroboam's son is comforting, 'He only shall come to the grave, because in him there is found some good thing toward the LORD God of Israel' (*1 Kings* 14:13), though only 'some good thing'. 'Lord, I believe' (*Mark* 9:24), with a weak faith, yet with faith; love thee with a faint love, yet with love; endeavour in a feeble manner, yet endeavour. A little fire is fire, though it smokes. Since thou hast taken me into thy covenant to be thine from being an enemy, wilt thou cast me off for these infirmities, which, as they displease thee, so are they the grief of my own heart?

8. *Duties and Discouragements*

From what has been said it will not be difficult, with a little further discussion, to resolve that question which some require help in, namely, whether we ought to perform duties when our hearts are altogether averse to them. To be satisfied on this point, we must take account of certain things.

WE SHOULD PERSIST IN DUTIES

1. *Our hearts of themselves are reluctant to give up their liberty,* and are only with difficulty brought under the yoke of duty. The more spiritual the duty is, the more reluctance there is. Corruption gains ground, for the most part, in every neglect. It is as in rowing against the tide, one stroke neglected will not be gained in three; and therefore it is good to keep our hearts close to duty, and not to listen to the excuses they are ready to frame.

2. *As we set about duty, God strengthens the influence that he has in us.* We find a warmness of heart and increase of strength, the Spirit going along with us and raising us up by degrees, until he leaves us as it were in heaven. God often delights to take advantage of our averseness, that he

may manifest his work the more clearly, and that all the glory of the work may be his, as all the strength is his.

3. *Obedience is most direct when there is nothing else to sweeten the action.* Although the sacrifice is imperfect, yet the obedience with which it is offered is accepted.

4. *What is won as a spoil from our corruptions will have as great a degree of comfort afterwards as it has of obstruction for the present.* Feeling and freeness of spirit are often reserved until duty is discharged. Reward follows work. In and after duty we find that experience of God's presence which, without obedience, we may long wait for, and yet go without. This does not hinder the Spirit's freedom in blowing upon our souls when he pleases (*John* 3:8), for we speak only of such a state of soul as is becalmed and must row, as it were, against the stream. As in sailing the hand must be to the helm and the eye to the star, so here we must put forth that little strength we have to duty and look up for assistance, which the Spirit, as freely as seasonably, will afford.

Yet in these duties that require the body as well as the soul there may be a cessation till strength is restored. Whetting a tool does not hinder, but prepares. In sudden passions, also, there should be a time to compose and calm the soul, and to put the strings in tune. The prophet asked for a minstrel to bring his soul into frame (*2 Kings* 3:15).

OVERCOMING DISCOURAGEMENTS

Suffering brings discouragements, because of our impatience. 'Alas!', we lament, 'I shall never get through such a trial.' But if God brings us into the trial he will be with us in the trial, and at length bring us out, more refined. We shall lose nothing but dross (*Zech.* 13:9). From our own strength we cannot bear the least trouble, but by the Spirit's assistance we can bear the greatest. The Spirit will add his shoulders to help us to bear our infirmities. The Lord will give his hand to heave us up (*Psa.* 37:24). 'Ye have heard of the patience of Job,' says James (*James* 5:11). We have heard of his impatience too, but it pleased God mercifully to overlook that. It yields us comfort also in desolate conditions, such as contagious sicknesses and the like, in which we are more immediately under God's hand, that then Christ has a throne of mercy at our bedside and numbers our tears and our groans. And, to come to the matter we are now about, the Sacrament[1], it was ordained not for angels, but for men; and not for perfect men, but for weak men; and not for Christ, who is truth itself, to bind him, but because we are ready, by reason of our guilty and unbelieving hearts, to call truth itself into question.

Therefore it was not enough for his goodness to leave us many precious promises, but he gives us confirming tokens to strengthen us. And even if we are not so prepared as we should be, yet let us pray as Hezekiah did: 'The good LORD pardon every one that prepareth his heart to seek God, the LORD God of his fathers, though he be not cleansed according to the purification of the sanctuary' (*2 Chron.* 30:18,19). Then we come comfortably to this holy sacrament, and with much fruit. This should carry us through all duties with much cheerfulness, that, if we hate our corruptions and strive against them, they shall not be counted ours. 'It is no more I that do it,' says Paul, 'but sin that dwelleth in me' (*Rom.* 7:17). For what displeases us shall never hurt us, and we shall be esteemed by God to be what we love and desire and labour to be. What we desire to be we shall be, and what

---

[1] A marginal note in early editions reads, 'This was preached at the Sacrament'.

we desire truly to conquer we shall conquer, for God will fulfil the desire of them that fear him (*Psa.* 145:19). The desire is an earnest of the thing desired. How little encouragement will carry us to the affairs of this life! And yet all the helps God offers will hardly prevail with our backward natures.

THE SOURCE OF DISCOURAGEMENTS

Where, then, do these discouragements come from?

1. *Not from the Father,* for he has bound himself in covenant to pity us as a father pities his children (*Psa.* 103:13) and to accept as a father our weak endeavours. And what is wanting in the strength of duty, he gives us leave to take up in his gracious indulgence. In this way we shall honour that grace in which he delights as much as in more perfect performances. *Possibilitas tua mensura tua* (What is possible to you is what you will be measured by).

2. *Not from Christ,* for he by office will not quench the smoking flax. We see how Christ bestows the best fruits of his love on persons who are mean in condition, weak in abilities, and offensive for infirmities, nay, for grosser falls. And this he does, first, because thus it pleases him to confound the pride of the flesh, which usually measures God's love by some outward excellency; and secondly, in this way he delights to show the freedom of his grace and confirm his royal prerogative that 'he that glorieth' must 'glory in the Lord' (*1 Cor.* 1:31).

In the eleventh chapter of Hebrews, among that cloud of witnesses, we see Rahab, Gideon and Samson ranked with Abraham, the father of the faithful (*Heb.* 11:31–32). Our blessed Saviour, as he was the image of his Father, so in this he was of the same mind, glorifying his Father for revealing the mystery of the gospel to simple men, neglecting those that carried the chief reputation of wisdom in the world (*Matt.* 11:25–26).

It is not unworthy of being recorded, what Augustine speaks of a simple man in his time, destitute almost altogether of the use of reason, who, although he was most patient of all injuries done to himself, yet from a reverence of religion he would not endure any injury done to the name of Christ, so much so that he would cast stones at those that blasphemed, not even sparing his own governors. This shows that none have abilities so meagre as to be beneath the gracious regard of Christ. Where it pleases him to make his choice and to exalt his mercy he passes by no degree of understanding, though never so simple.

3.   *Neither do discouragements come from the Spirit.* He helps our infirmities, and by office is a comforter (*Rom.* 8:26; *John* 14:16). If he convinces of sin, and so humbles us, it is that he may make way for his office of comforting us. Discouragements, then, must come from ourselves and from Satan, who labours to fasten on us a loathing of duty.

SOME SCRUPLES REMOVED

Among other causes of discouragement, some are much vexed with scruples, even against the best duties; partly by disease of body, helped by Satan's malice in casting dust in their eyes in their way to heaven; and partly from some remainder of ignorance, which, like darkness, breeds fears – ignorance especially of this merciful disposition in Christ, the persuasion of which would easily banish false fears. They conceive of him as one on watch for all advantages against them, in which they may see how they wrong not only themselves but his goodness. This scrupulosity, for the most part, is a sign of a godly soul, as some weeds are of a good soil. Therefore they are the more to be pitied, for it is a heavy affliction, and the ground of it in most is not so much from trouble of conscience as from a disordered imagination. The end of Christ's coming was to free us from all such groundless fears. There is still in some such ignorance of that comfortable condition we are in under the covenant of grace as to discourage them greatly. Therefore we must understand that:

1. *Weaknesses do not break covenant with God.* They do not break the covenant between husband and wife, and shall we make ourselves more pitiful than Christ who makes himself a pattern of love to all other husbands?

2. *Weaknesses do not debar us from mercy*; rather they incline God to us the more (*Psa.* 78:39). Mercy is a part of the church's marriage inheritance. Christ betroths her to him 'in mercy' (*Hos.* 2:19). The husband is bound to bear with the wife, as being the 'weaker vessel' (*1 Pet.* 3:7), and shall we think Christ will exempt himself from his own rule, and not bear with his weak spouse?

3. *If Christ should not be merciful to our weaknesses, he should not have a people to serve him.* Suppose therefore we are very weak, yet so long as we are not found amongst malicious opposers and underminers of God's truth, let us not give way to despairing thoughts; we have a merciful Saviour.

But lest we flatter ourselves without good grounds, we must know that weaknesses are to be reckoned either imperfections cleaving to our best actions, or actions proceeding from immaturity in Christ, whilst we are babes, or the effects of want of strength, where ability is small, or sudden unintended breakings out, contrary to our general bent and purpose, whilst our judgment is overcast with the cloud of a sudden temptation, after which we feel our infirmity, grieve for it and from grief, complain, and, with complaining, strive and labour to reform; finally, in labouring, we make some progress against our corruption.

Weaknesses so considered, although a matter of humiliation and the object of our daily mortification, yet may be consistent with boldness with God, nor is a good work either extinguished by them or tainted so far as to lose all acceptance with God. But to plead for an infirmity is more than an infirmity; to allow ourselves in weaknesses is more than a weakness. The justification of evil shuts our mouths, so that the soul cannot call God Father with child-like liberty, or enjoy sweet communion with him, until peace be made by shaming ourselves, and renewing our faith. Those that have ever been bruised for sin, if they fall, are soon recovered. Peter was recovered with a gracious look of Christ, David by Abigail's words. If you tell a thief or a vagrant that he is out of the way, he pays no heed, because his aim is not to walk in any particular way, except as it suits his purpose.

WHAT ARE SINS OF INFIRMITY?

To clarify this further, we must understand that:

1. *Wherever sins of infirmity are in a person, there must be the life of grace begun.* There can be no weakness where there is no life.

2. *There must be a sincere and general bent to the best things.* Though a godly man may suddenly be drawn or driven aside in some particulars, yet, by reason of that interest the Spirit of Christ has in him, and because his aims are right in the main, he will either recover of himself, or yield to the counsel of others.

3. *There must be a right judgment, allowing of the best ways, or else the heart is rotten.* Then it will infuse corruption into the whole conversation, so that all men's actions become

infected at the spring-head. They then justify looseness and condemn God's ways as too much strictness. Their principles whereby they work are not good.

4.   *There must be a conjugal love to Christ,* so that there are no terms on which they will change their Lord and husband, and yield themselves absolutely over to be ruled by their own lusts, or the lusts of others.

A Christian's behaviour towards Christ may in many things be very offensive, and cause some strangeness; yet he will own Christ, and Christ him; he will not resolve upon any way wherein he knows he must break with Christ. Where the heart is thus in these respects qualified, there we must know this, that Christ counts it his honour to pass by many infirmities, nay, in infirmities he perfects his strength. There are some almost invincible infirmities, such as forgetfulness, heaviness of spirit, sudden passions and fears which, though natural, yet are for the most part tainted with sin. Of these, if the life of Christ be in us, we are weary, and would fain shake them off, as a sick man his fever; otherwise it is not to be esteemed weakness so much as wilfulness, and the more will, the more sin. And little sins, when God shall awaken the conscience and 'set them in order' before us (*Psa.* 50:21) will prove great burdens, and not only bruise a reed, but shake a cedar. Yet God's children never sin with full will, because there is a contrary law in their minds by which the dominion of sin is broken and which always has some secret working against the law of sin. Nevertheless there may be so much will in a sinful action as may destroy our comfort to a remarkable degree afterwards and keep us long on the rack of a disquieted conscience, God in his fatherly dispensation suspending the sense of his love. To the extent that we give way to our will in sinning, to that extent we set ourselves at a distance from comfort. Sin against conscience is as a thief[2] in the candle, which spoils our joy, and thereby weakens our strength. We must know, therefore, that wilful breaches in sanctification will much hinder the sense of our justification.

What course shall such take to recover their peace? They must condemn themselves sharply, and yet cast themselves upon God's mercy in Christ, as at their first conversion. And now they must embrace Christ the more firmly, as they see more need in themselves; and let them remember the mildness of Christ here, that he will not quench the smoking flax. Often we see that, after a deep humiliation, Christ speaks more peace than before, to witness the truth of this reconciliation, because he knows Satan's enterprises in casting such down lower, because they are most abased in themselves and are ashamed to look Christ in the face, because of their ingratitude.

We see that God did not only pardon David but, after much bruising, gave him wise Solomon to succeed him in the kingdom. We see in Song of Solomon 6:4 that, after the church has been humbled for her slighting of Christ, he sweetly entertains her again, and begins to commend her beauty. We must know for our comfort that Christ was not anointed to this great work of Mediator for lesser sins only, but for the greatest, if we have but a spark of true faith to lay hold on him. Therefore, if there be any bruised reed, let him not make an exception of himself, when Christ does not make an exception of him. 'Come unto me, *all* ye that labour and are heavy laden' (*Matt.* 11:28). Why should we not make use of so gracious a disposition? We are only poor for this reason, that we do not know our riches in Christ. In time of temptation, believe Christ rather than the devil. Believe truth from truth itself. Hearken not to a liar, an enemy and a murderer.

[2] A flaw in a candle wick which causes guttering.

9. *Believe Christ, Not Satan*

Since Christ is thus comfortably set out to us, let us not believe Satan's representations of him. When we are troubled in conscience for our sins, Satan's manner is then to present Christ to the afflicted soul as a most severe judge armed with justice against us. But then let us present him to our souls as offered to our view by God himself, holding out a sceptre of mercy, and spreading his arms to receive us.

HOW WE SHOULD THINK OF CHRIST

When we think of Joseph, Daniel, John the Evangelist, we frame conceptions of them with delight, as of mild and sweet persons. Much more when we think of Christ, we should conceive of him as a mirror of all meekness. If the sweetness of all flowers were in one, how sweet must that flower be? In Christ all perfections of mercy and love meet. How great then must that mercy be that lodges in so gracious a heart? Whatever tenderness is scattered in husband, father, brother, head, all is but a beam from him; it is in him in the most eminent manner. We are weak, but we are his; we are deformed, but yet carry his image upon us. A father looks not so much at the blemishes of his child as at his own nature in him; so Christ finds matter of love from that which is his own in us. He sees his own nature in us: we are diseased, but yet his members. Who ever neglected his own members because they were sick or weak? None ever hated his own flesh. Can the head forget the members? Can Christ forget himself? We are his fulness, as he is ours. He was love itself clothed with man's nature, which he united so near to himself, that he might communicate his goodness the more freely to us. And he took not our nature when it was at its best, but when it was abased, with all the natural and common infirmities it was subject to.

Let us therefore abhor all suspicious thoughts, as either cast in or cherished by that damned spirit who, as he laboured to divide between the Father and the Son by jealousies, by saying, 'If thou be the Son of God' (*Matt.* 4:6), so his daily study is to divide between the Son and us by breeding false opinions in us of Christ, as if there were not such tender love in him to such as we are. It was Satan's art from the beginning to discredit God with man, by calling God's love into question with our first father Adam. His success then makes him ready at that weapon still.

WHEN CHRIST SEEMS TO BE AN ENEMY

'But for all this, I feel not Christ so to me,' says the smoking flax, 'but rather the clean contrary. He seems to be an enemy to me. I see and feel evidences of his just displeasure.'

Christ may act the part of an enemy a little while, as Joseph did, but it is to make way for acting his own part of mercy in a more seasonable time. He cannot restrain his bowels of mercy long. He seems to wrestle with us, as with Jacob, but he supplies us with hidden strength to prevail at length. Faith pulls off the mask from his face and sees a loving heart under contrary appearances. *Fides Christo larvam detrahit* (Faith pulls away the mask from Christ). At first he answered the woman of Canaan, who was crying after him, not a word. Then he gave her a denial. After that he gave an answer tending to her reproach, calling her a dog, as being outside the covenant. Yet she would not be so beaten off, for she considered the end of his coming. As his Father was never nearer him in strength to support him than when he was furthest off in sense of favour to comfort him, so Christ is never nearer us in power to uphold us than when he seems most to hide his presence from us. The influence of the Sun of righteousness pierces deeper than his light. In such cases, whatever Christ's present bearing is towards us, let us oppose his nature and office against it. He cannot deny himself, he cannot but discharge the office his Father has laid upon him. We see here the Father has undertaken that he shall not 'quench the smoking flax', and Christ has also undertaken to represent us to the Father, appearing before him for us until he presents us blameless before him (*John* 17:6,11). The Father has given us to Christ, and Christ gives us back again to the Father.

WHEN DOUBT ASSAILS US

'This would be good comfort,' says one, 'if I were but as smoking flax.'

It is well that this objection pinches on yourself, and not on Christ. It is well that you give him the honour of his mercy towards others, though not to yourself. Yet do not wrong the work of his Spirit in your heart. Satan, as he slanders Christ to us, so he slanders us to ourselves. If you are not so much as smoking flax, then why do you not renounce your interest in Christ, and disclaim the covenant of grace? This you dare not do. Why do you not give yourself up wholly to other pleasures? This your spirit will not allow you to do. Where do these restless groanings and complaints come from? Lay your present state alongside the office of Christ to such, and do not despise the consolation of the Almighty nor refuse your own mercy. Cast yourself into the arms of Christ, and if you perish, perish there. If you do not, you are sure to perish. If mercy is to be found anywhere, it is there.

In this appears Christ's care to you, that he has given you a heart in some degree sensitive. He might have given you up to hardness, security and profaneness of heart, of all spiritual judgments the greatest. He who died for his enemies, will he refuse those, the desire of whose soul is towards him? He who, by his messengers, desires us to be reconciled, will he put us off when we earnestly seek it at his hand? No, doubtless, when he goes before us by kindling holy desires in us, he is ready to meet us in his own ways. When the prodigal set himself to return to his father, his father did not wait for him, but met him in the way. When he prepares the heart to seek, he causes his ear to hear (*Psa.* 10:17). He cannot find in his heart to hide himself long from us. If God should bring us into such a dark condition as that we should see no light from himself or the creature, then let us remember what he says by the prophet Isaiah, 'Who is among you . . . that walketh in darkness, and hath no light?' – no light of comfort, no light of God's countenance – 'let him trust in the name of the LORD, and stay upon his God' (*Isa.* 50:10). We can never be in such a condition that there will be just cause of utter despair. Therefore let us do as mariners do, cast anchor in the dark. Christ knows how to pity us in this case. Look what comfort he felt from his

Father when he was broken (*Isa.* 53:5). This is what we shall feel from himself in our bruising.

The sighs of a bruised heart carry in them a report, both of our affection to Christ, and of his care to us. The eyes of our souls cannot be towards him unless he has cast a gracious look upon us first. The least love we have to him is but a reflection of his love first shining upon us. As Christ did, in his example to us, whatever he charges us to do, so he suffered in his own person whatever he calls us to suffer, so that he might the better learn to relieve and pity us in our sufferings. In his desertion in the garden and on the cross he was content to be without that unspeakable solace which the presence of his Father gave, both to bear the wrath of the Lord for a time for us, and likewise to know the better how to comfort us in our greatest extremities. God sees fit that we should taste of that cup of which his Son drank so deep, that we might feel a little what sin is, and what his Son's love was. But our comfort is that Christ drank the dregs of the cup for us, and will succour us, so that our spirits may not utterly fail under that little taste of his displeasure which we may feel. He became not only a man but a curse, a man of sorrows, for us. He was broken that we should not be broken; he was troubled, that we should not be desperately troubled; he became a curse, that we should not be accursed. Whatever may be wished for in an all-sufficient comforter is all to be found in Christ:

1. *Authority from the Father.* All power was given to him (*Matt.* 28:18).

2. *Strength in himself.* His name is 'The mighty God' (*Isa.* 9:6).

3. *Wisdom,* and that from his own experience, how and when to help (*Heb.* 2:18).

4. *Willingness,* as being bone of our bones and flesh of our flesh (*Gen.* 2:23; *Eph.* 5:30).

10. *Quench Not the Spirit*

We are now to take notice of various sorts of men that offend deeply against this merciful disposition of Christ.

FALSE DESPAIR OF CHRIST'S MERCY

There are those who go on in all ill courses of life on this pretence, that it would be useless to go to Christ, because their lives have been so bad; whereas, as soon as we look to heaven, all encouragements are ready to meet us and draw us forward. Among others, this is one allurement, that Christ is ready to welcome us and lead us further. None are damned in the church but those that are determined to be, including those who persist in having hard thoughts of Christ, that they may have some show of reason to fetch contentment from other things, as that unprofitable servant (*Matt.* 25:30) who would needs take up the opinion that his master was a hard man, thereby to flatter himself in his unfruitful ways, in not improving the talent which he had.

FALSE HOPE OF CHRIST'S MERCY

There are those who take up a hope of their own, that Christ will suffer them to walk in the ways to hell, and yet bring them to heaven; whereas all comfort should draw us nearer to Christ. Otherwise it is a lying comfort, either in itself or in our application of it.

RESISTING CHRIST'S MERCY

There are those who take it on themselves to cast water on those sparks which Christ labours to kindle in them, because they will not be troubled with the light of them. Such must know that the Lamb can be angry, and that they who will not come under his sceptre of mercy shall be crushed in pieces by his sceptre of power (*Psa.* 2:9). Though he will graciously tend and maintain the least spark of true grace, yet where he finds not the spark of grace but opposition to his Spirit striving with them, his wrath, once kindled, shall burn to hell. There is no more just provocation than when kindness is churlishly refused.

When God would have cured Babylon, and she would not be cured, then she was given up to destruction (*Jer.* 51:9). When Jerusalem would not be gathered under the wing of Christ, then their habitation is left desolate (*Matt.* 23:37,38). When wisdom stretches out her hand and men refuse, then wisdom will laugh at men's destruction (*Prov.* 1:26). Salvation itself will not save those that spill the medicine and cast away the plaster. It is a pitiful case, when this merciful Saviour shall delight in destruction; when he that made men shall have no mercy on them (*Isa.* 27:11).

Oh, say the rebels of the time, God has not made us to damn us. Yes, if you will not meet Christ in the ways of his mercy, it is fitting that you should 'eat of the fruit of your own way, and be filled with your own devices' (*Prov.* 1:31). This will be the hell of hell, when men shall think that they have loved their sins more than their souls; when they shall think what love and mercy has been almost enforced upon them, and yet they would perish. The more accessory we are in pulling a judgment upon ourselves, the more the conscience will be confounded in itself. Then they shall acknowledge Christ to be without any blame, themselves without any excuse.

If men appeal to their own consciences, they will tell them that the Holy Spirit has often knocked at their hearts, as willing to have kindled some holy desires in them. How else can they be said to resist the Holy Ghost, but that the Spirit was readier to draw them to a further degree of goodness than was consistent with their own wills? Therefore those in the church that are damned are self-condemned before. So that here we need not rise to higher causes, when men carry sufficient cause in their own bosoms.

PRESUMING ON CHRIST'S MERCY

And the best of us all may offend against this merciful disposition if we are not watchful against that liberty which our carnal disposition will be ready to take from it. Thus we reason, if Christ will not quench the smoking flax, what need we fear that any neglect on our part can bring us into a comfortless condition? If Christ will not do it, what can?

You know the apostle's prohibition, notwithstanding, 'Quench not the Spirit' (*1 Thess.* 5:19). Such cautions of not quenching are sanctified by the Spirit as a means of not quenching. Christ performs his office in not quenching by stirring up suitable endeavours in us; and there are none more solicitous in the use of the means than those that are most certain of their good success. The reason is this: the means that God has set apart for the effecting of any thing are included in the purpose that he has to bring that thing to pass. And this is a principle taken for granted, even in civil matters; for who, if he knew before that it would be a fruitful year, would therefore hang up his plough and neglect tillage?

Hence the apostle stirs us up from the certain expectation of a blessing (*1 Cor.* 15:57,58), and this encouragement from the good issue of victory is intended to stir us up, and not to put us off. If we are negligent in the exercise of grace received and the use of the means prescribed, suffering our spirits to be oppressed with many and various cares of this life, and take not heed of the discouragements of the times, for this kind of neglect God in his wise care suffers us often to fall into a worse condition in our feelings than those that were never so much enlightened. Yet in mercy he will not suffer us to be so far enemies to ourselves as wholly to neglect these sparks once kindled. Were it possible that we should be given up to abandon all endeavour wholly, then we could look for no other issue but quenching; but Christ will tend this spark and cherish this small seed, so that he will always preserve in the soul some degree of care.

If we would make a comfortable use of this, we must consider all those means whereby Christ preserves grace begun; such as, first, holy communion, by which one Christian warms another. 'Two are better than one' (*Eccles.* 4:9). 'Did not our heart burn within us?', said the disciples (*Luke* 24:32). Secondly, much more communion with God in holy duties, such as meditation and prayer, which not only kindles but adds a lustre to the soul. Thirdly, we feel by experience the breath of the Spirit to go along with the breath of his ministers. For this reason the apostle knits these two together: 'Quench not the Spirit. Despise not prophesyings' (*1 Thess.* 5:19,20). Nathan, by a few words, blew up the decaying sparks in David. Rather than that God will suffer his fire in us to die, he will send some Nathan or other, and something always is left in us to join with the Word, as of the same nature with it; as a coal that has fire in it will quickly gather more fire to it. Smoking flax will easily take fire. Fourthly, grace is strengthened by the exercise of it: 'Arise therefore, and be doing, and the LORD be with thee' (*1 Chron.* 22:16), said David to his son Solomon. Stir up the grace that is in you, for in this way holy motions turn to resolutions, resolutions to practice, and practice to a prepared readiness to every good work.

However, let us remember that grace is increased, in the exercise of it, not by virtue of the exercise itself, but as Christ by his Spirit flows into the soul and brings us nearer to himself, the fountain, so instilling such comfort that the heart is further enlarged. The heart of a Christian is Christ's garden, and his graces are as so many sweet spices and flowers which, when his Spirit blows upon them, send forth a sweet savour. Therefore keep the soul open to entertain the Holy Ghost, for he will bring in continually fresh forces to subdue corruption, and this most of all on the Lord's day. John was in the Spirit on the Lord's day, even in Patmos, the place of his banishment (*Rev.* 1:10). Then the gales of the Spirit blow more strongly and sweetly.

As we look, therefore, for the comfort of this doctrine, let us not favour our natural sloth but exercise ourselves rather to godliness (*1 Tim.* 4:7), and labour to keep this fire always burning upon the altar of our hearts. Let us dress our lamps daily, and put in fresh oil, and wind up our souls higher and higher still. Resting in a good condition is contrary to grace, which cannot but promote itself to a further measure. Let none turn this grace 'into lasciviousness' (*Jude* 4). Infirmities are a ground of humility, not a plea for negligence, nor an encouragement to presumption. We should be so far from being evil because Christ is good that those coals of love should melt us. Therefore those may well suspect themselves in whom the consideration of this mildness of Christ does not work that way. Surely where grace is, corruption is 'as vinegar to the teeth, and as smoke to the eyes' (*Prov.* 10:26). And therefore they will labour, with respect to their own comfort, as likewise for the credit of religion and the glory of God, that their light may break forth. If a spark of faith and love is so precious, what an honour will it be to be rich in faith! Who would not rather walk in the light, and in the comforts of the Holy Ghost, than live in a dark, perplexed state? And not rather be carried with full sail to heaven than be tossed always with fears and doubts? The present trouble in conflict against a sin is not so much as that disquiet which any corruption favoured will bring upon us afterward. True peace is in conquering, not in yielding. The comfort intended in this text is for those that would fain do better, but find their corruptions clog them; that are in such a mist, that often they cannot tell what to think of themselves; that fain would believe, and yet often fear that they do not believe; and that think that it cannot be that God should be so good to such sinful wretches as they are, and yet they do not permit these fears and doubts in themselves.

SEEKING ANOTHER SOURCE OF MERCY

And among others, how do they wrong themselves and him that will have other mediators to God for them than he! Are any more pitiful than he who became man to that end, that he might be pitiful to his own flesh? Let all, at all times, repair to this meek Saviour, and put up all our petitions in his prevailing name. What need do we have to knock at any other door? Can any be more tender over us than Christ? What encouragement we have to commend the state of the church in general, or of any broken-hearted Christian, to him by our prayers, of whom we may speak to Christ, as they did of Lazarus, 'Lord, the church which thou lovest, and gavest thyself for, is in distress'; 'Lord, this poor Christian, for whom thou wast bruised (*Isa.* 53:5) is bruised and brought very low.' It cannot but touch his heart when the misery of those so dear to him is spread before him.

MISTREATING THE HEIRS OF MERCY

Again, considering this gracious nature in Christ, let us think with ourselves thus: when he is so kind to us, shall we be cruel against him in his name, in his truth, in his children? How shall those that delight to be so terrible to 'the meek of the earth' (*Zeph.* 2:3) hope to look so gracious a Saviour in the face? They that are so boisterous towards his spouse shall know one day that they had to deal with himself in his church. So it cannot but cut the heart of those that have felt this love of Christ to hear him wounded who is the life of their lives and the soul of their souls. This makes those that have felt mercy weep over Christ whom they have pierced with their sins. There cannot but be a mutual and quick sympathy between the head and the members. When we are tempted to any sin, if we will not pity ourselves, yet we should spare Christ, in not putting him to new torments. The apostle could not find out a more heart-breaking argument to enforce a sacrifice of ourselves to God than to appeal to us 'by the mercies of God' in Christ (*Rom.* 12:1).

STRIFE AMONG THE HEIRS OF MERCY

This mercy of Christ should also move us to commiserate the state of the poor church, torn by enemies without, and rending itself by divisions at home. It cannot but affect any soul that ever felt comfort from Christ to consider what an affectionate entreaty the apostle makes to mutual agreement in judgment and affection. 'If there be therefore any consolation in Christ, if any comfort of love, if any fellowship of the Spirit, if any bowels and mercies, fulfil ye my joy, that ye be like-minded' (*Phil.* 2:1), as if he should say, 'Unless you will disclaim all consolation in Christ, labour to maintain the unity of the Spirit in the bond of peace.' What a joyful spectacle is this to Satan and his faction, to see those that are separated from the world fall in pieces among themselves! Our discord is our enemy's melody.

The more to blame are those that for private aims affect differences from others, and will not suffer the wounds of the church to close and meet together. This must not be understood as if men should dissemble their judgment in any truth where there is just cause of expressing themselves; for the least truth is Christ's and not ours, and therefore we are not to take liberty to affirm or deny at our pleasure. There is something due on a penny as well as on a pound, therefore we must be faithful in the least truth, when the season calls for it. Then our words are 'like apples of gold in pictures of silver' (*Prov.* 25:11). One word spoken in season will do more good than a thousand out of season. But in some cases peace, through having our faith to ourselves before God (*Rom.* 14:22), is of more consequence than the open discovery of some things we take to be true, considering that the weakness of man's nature is such that there can hardly be a discovery of any difference in opinion without some estrangement of affection. So far as men are not of one mind, they will hardly be of one heart, except where grace and the peace of God bear great rule in the heart (*Col.* 3:15). Therefore open show of difference is only good when it is necessary, although some, from a desire to be somebody, turn into by-ways and yield to a spirit of contradiction in themselves. Yet, if Paul may be judge, they 'are yet carnal' (*1 Cor.* 3:3). If it be wisdom, it is wisdom from beneath: for the wisdom from above, as it is pure, so it is peaceable (*James* 3:17). Our blessed Saviour, when he was to leave the world, what did he press upon his disciples more than peace and love? And in his last prayer, with what earnestness did he beg of his Father that 'they all may be one', as he and the Father were one (*John* 17:21). But what he prayed for on earth, we shall only enjoy perfectly in heaven. Let this make the meditation of that time the more sweet unto us.

TAKING ADVANTAGE OF THE BRUISED

And further, to expose offenders of this kind, what spirit shall we think them to be of that take advantage of the bruisedness and infirmities of men's spirits to relieve them with false peace for their own worldly ends? A wounded spirit will part with anything. Most of the gainful points of popery, such as confession, satisfaction, merit and purgatory, spring from hence, but they are physicians of no value, or tormentors and not physicians at all. It is a greater blessing to be delivered from the sting of these scorpions (*Rev.* 9:5) than we are thankful for. Spiritual tyranny is the greatest tyranny, and then especially when it is where most mercy should be shown; yet even there some, like cruel surgeons, delight in making long cures, to serve themselves through the misery of others. It brings men under a terrible curse that they 'remembered not to shew mercy, but persecuted the poor and needy man', that they might 'even slay the broken in heart' (*Psa.* 109:16).

In the same way, to such as raise temporal advantage to themselves out of the spiritual misery of others we must add such as raise estates by betraying the church, and are unfaithful in the trust committed unto them, when the children cry for the bread of life, and there is none to give them, bringing thus upon the people of God that heavy judgment of a spiritual famine, starving Christ in his members. Shall we so requite so good a Saviour who counts the love and mercy shown in feeding his lambs (*John* 21:15) as shown to himself?

DESPISING THE SIMPLE MEANS OF MERCY

Lastly, they carry themselves very unkindly towards Christ who stumble at his low stooping to us in his government and ordinances, that are ashamed of the simplicity of the gospel, that count preaching foolishness. They, out of the pride of their heart, think that they may do well enough without the help of the Word and sacraments, and think Christ did not take enough dignity upon him; and therefore they will mend the matter with their own devices so that they may give better satisfaction to flesh and blood, as in popery. What greater unthankfulness can there be than to despise any help that Christ in mercy has provided for us? In the days of his flesh the proud Pharisees took offence at his familiar conversing with sinful men, though he only did so as a physician to heal their souls. What defences was Paul driven to make for himself, for his plainness in unfolding the gospel? The more Christ, in himself and in his servants, shall descend to exalt us, the more we should, with all humility and readiness, entertain that love and magnify the goodness of God, that has put the great work of our salvation, and laid the government, upon so gentle a Saviour as will carry himself so mildly in all things wherein he is to deal between God and us, and us and God. The lower Christ comes down to us, the higher let us lift him up in our hearts. So will all those do that have ever found the experience of Christ's work in their hearts.

11. *Christ's Judgment and Victory*

We come now to the last part of our text, concerning the constant progress of Christ's gracious power, until he has set up an absolute government in us which shall prevail over all corruptions. It is said here that he will cherish his beginnings of grace in us until he bring forth 'judgment unto victory' (*Matt.* 12:20).

CHRIST'S JUDGMENT ESTABLISHED IN US

By judgment here is meant the kingdom of grace in us, that government whereby Christ sets up a throne in our hearts. Governors among the Jews were first called judges, then kings, whence this inward rule is called judgment, as also because it agrees with the judgment of the Word, which the Psalmist often calls judgment (as in Psalm 72:1,2) because it agrees with God's judgment. Men may read their doom in God's Word. What it judges of them God judges of them. By this judgment set up in us, good is discerned, allowed, and performed; sin is judged, condemned, and executed. Our spirit, being under the Spirit of Christ, is governed by him, and, so far as it is governed by Christ, it governs us graciously.

Christ and we are of one judgment and of one will. He has his will in us, and his judgments are so invested with authority in us as that they are turned into our judgment, we carrying his law in our hearts, written there by his Spirit (*Jer.* 31:33). The law in the inner man and the law written answer to each other as counterparts.

The meaning then is that the gracious frame of holiness set up in our hearts by the Spirit of Christ shall go forward until all contrary power is subdued. The spirit of judgment will be a spirit of burning (*Isa.* 4:4) to consume whatever opposed corruption eats into the soul like rust. If God's builders fall into errors and build stubble on a good foundation, God's Spirit, as a spiritual fire, will reveal this in time (*1 Cor.* 3:13), and destroy it. The builders shall, by a spirit of judgment, condemn their own errors and courses. The whole work of grace in us is set out under the name of judgment, and sometimes wisdom, because judgment is the chief and leading part in grace, so that the gracious work of repentance is called a change of the mind, and an after-wisdom. On the other hand, in the learned languages the words that express wisdom imply also a general relish and savour of the whole soul, and rather more the judgment of taste than of sight or any other sense, because taste is the most necessary sense, and requires a nearer application of the object than all other senses. So, in spiritual life, it is most necessary that the Spirit should alter the taste of the soul so that it might savour the things of the Spirit so deeply that all other things should be out of relish.

And as it is true of every particular Christian that Christ's judgment in him shall be victorious, so likewise of the whole body of Christians, the church. The government of Christ, and his truth, whereby he rules as by a sceptre, shall at length be victorious in spite of Satan, antichrist, and all enemies. Christ, riding on his white horse (*Rev.* 6:2), has a bow and goes forth conquering, in the ministry, that he may overcome either to conversion or to confusion. But yet I take judgment principally for Christ's kingdom and government within us, firstly, because God especially requires the subjection of the soul and conscience as his proper throne; and, secondly, because, if judgment should prevail in all others about us and not in our own hearts, it would not yield comfort to us; and therefore it is the first thing that we desire when we pray, 'Thy kingdom come', that Christ would come and rule in our hearts. The kingdom of Christ in his ordinances serves but to bring Christ home into his own place, our hearts.

The words being thus explained, that judgment here includes the government of mind, will and affections, there are various conclusions that naturally spring from them.

CHRIST'S MILDNESS AND HIS GOVERNMENT

The first conclusion from the connection of this part of the verse with the former is that Christ is mild in the way that we have seen so that he may then set up his government in those whom he is so gentle and tender over. He pardons in this way so as to be obeyed as a king; he takes us to be his spouse so as to be obeyed as a husband. The same Spirit that convinces us of the necessity of his righteousness to cover us convinces us also of the necessity of his government to rule us. His love to us moves him to frame us to be like himself, and our love to him stirs us up to be such as he may take delight in, neither do we have faith or hope any further than we have a concern to be purged as he is pure. He makes us subordinate governors, yea, kings under himself, giving us grace not only to fight but to subdue in some measure our base affections. It is one main fruit of Christ's exaltation that he may turn every one of us from our wickedness (*Acts* 3:26). 'For to this end Christ both died, and rose, and revived, that he might be Lord both of the dead and living' (*Rom.*14:9). God has bound himself by an oath that he would grant us that 'we might serve him without fear, in holiness and righteousness before him' (*Luke* 1:75), and not only before the world.

PARDON LEADS TO OBEDIENCE

This may serve for a trial to discern who may lay just claim to Christ's mercy. Only those that will take his yoke and count it a greater happiness to be under his government than to enjoy any liberty of the flesh; that will take whole Christ, and not single out of him what may stand with their present contentment; that will not divide Lord from Jesus, and so make a Christ of their own, may make this claim. None ever did truly desire mercy for pardon but desired mercy for healing. David prays for a new spirit, as well as for a sense of pardoning mercy (*Psa.* 51:10).

JUSTIFICATION LEADS TO SANCTIFICATION

This also shows that those are misled that make Christ to be only righteousness to us and not sanctification, except by imputation, whereas it is a great part of our happiness to be under such a Lord, who was not only born for us, and given to us, but has the government likewise upon his shoulder (*Isa.* 9:6,7). He is our Sanctifier as well as our Saviour, our Saviour as well by the effectual power of his Spirit from the power of sin as by the merit of his death from the guilt thereof; provided these things are remembered:

1. The first and chief ground of our comfort is that Christ as a priest offered himself as a sacrifice to his Father for us. The guilty soul flies first to Christ crucified, made a curse for us. Thence it is that Christ has right to govern us; thence it is that he gives us his Spirit as our guide to lead us home.

2. In the course of our life, after we are in a state of grace, if we are overtaken with any sin, we must remember to have recourse first to Christ's mercy to pardon us, and then to the promise of his Spirit to govern us.

3. And when we feel ourselves cold in affection and duty, the best way is to warm ourselves at this fire of his love and mercy in giving himself for us.

4. Again, remember this, that Christ rules us by a spirit of love, from a sense of his love, whereby his commandments are easy to us. He leads us by his free Spirit, a Spirit of liberty. His subjects are voluntaries. The constraint that he lays upon his subjects is that of love. He draws us sweetly with the cords of love. Yet remember also that he draws us strongly by a Spirit of power, for it is not sufficient that we have motives and encouragements to love and obey Christ from that love of his, whereby he gave himself for us to justify us; but Christ's Spirit must likewise subdue our hearts, and sanctify them to love him, without which all motives would be ineffectual.

Our disposition must be changed. We must be new creatures. They seek for heaven in hell that seek for spiritual love in an unchanged heart. When a child obeys his father it is from reasons persuading him, as likewise from a child-like nature which gives strength to these reasons. It is natural for a child of God to love Christ so far as he is renewed, not only from inducement of reason so to do, but likewise from an inward principle and work of grace, whence those reasons have their chief force. First we are made partakers of the divine nature, and then we are easily induced and led by Christ's Spirit to spiritual duties.

12. Christ's Wise Government

The second conclusion from the final part of the text is that Christ's government in his church and in his children is a wise and well-ordered government because it is called judgment, and judgment is the life and soul of wisdom. Of this conclusion there are two branches: first, that the spiritual government of Christ in us is joined with judgment and wisdom, and secondly, wherever true spiritual wisdom and judgment are, there likewise the Spirit of Christ has brought in his gracious government.

JUDGMENT AND WISDOM

As to the first, a well-guided life by the rules of Christ stands with the strongest and highest reason of all; and therefore holy men are called 'wisdom's children' (*Luke* 7:35), and are able to justify, both by reason and experience, all the ways of wisdom. Opposite courses are folly and madness. Hereupon Paul says that 'he that is spiritual judgeth all things' (*1 Cor.* 2:15) that appertain to him, and is judged of none that are of an inferior rank, because they lack spiritual light and sight to judge. Yet this sort of men will judge and 'speak evil of the things that they understand not' (*2 Pet.* 2:12); they step from ignorance to prejudice and rash censure, without taking right judgment in their way, and therefore their judgment comes to nothing. But the judgment of a spiritual man, so far as he is spiritual, shall stand, because it is agreeable to the nature of things. As things are in themselves, so they are in his judgment. As God is in himself infinite in goodness and majesty, so he is to him. He ascribes to God in his heart his divinity and all his excellencies. As Christ is in himself the only Mediator, and all in all in the church (*Col.* 3:11), so he is to him, by making Christ so in his heart. As all things are dung in comparison with Christ (*Phil.* 3:8), so they are to Paul, a sanctified man. As the very worst thing in religion, 'the reproach of Christ', is better than 'the pleasures of sin for a season' (*Heb.* 11:25–26), so it is to Moses, a man of a right esteem. As one day in the courts of God is better than a thousand elsewhere (*Psa.* 84:10), so it is to David, a man of a reformed judgment. There is a conformity of a good man's judgment to things as they are in themselves, and according to the difference or agreement put by God in things, so does his judgment differ or agree.

Truth is truth, and error, error, and that which is unlawful is unlawful, whether men think so or not. God has put an eternal difference between light and darkness, good and ill, which no creature's conceit can alter; and therefore no man's judgment is the measure of things further than it agrees to truth stamped upon things themselves by God. For this reason, because a wise man's judgment agrees to the truth of things, a wise man may in some sense be said to be the measure of things, and the judgment of one holy wise man to be preferred before a thousand others. Such men usually are immovable as the sun in its course, because they think, and speak and live by rule. A Joshua and his house will serve God (*Josh.* 24:15), whatsoever others do, and will run a course contrary to the world, because their judgments lead them a contrary way. Hence it is that Satan has a spite at the eye of the soul, the judgment, to put it out by ignorance and false reason, for he cannot rule in any until either he has taken away or perverted judgment. He is a prince of darkness, and rules in darkness of the understanding. Therefore he must first be cast out of the understanding by the prevailing of truth and planting of it in the soul. Those, therefore, that are enemies of knowledge help Satan and antichrist, whose kingdom, like Satan's, is a kingdom of darkness, to erect their throne. Hence it is promised by Christ, that the Holy Ghost shall convince the world of righteousness or judgment (*John* 16:8); that is, that he is resolved to set up a throne of government, because the great lord of misrule, Satan, 'the prince of this world', is judged by the gospel, and the Spirit accompanying it. His impostures are discovered, his enterprises laid open. Therefore when the gospel was spread the oracles ceased, Satan fell from heaven like lightning (*Luke* 10:18). Men were translated out of his kingdom into Christ's. Where prevailing is by lies, discovery is victory: 'they shall proceed no further: for their folly shall be manifest unto all men' (*2 Tim.* 3:9). So that manifestation of error gives a stop to it, for none will willingly be deceived. Let truth have full scope without check or restraint, and let Satan and his instruments do their worst, they shall not prevail, as Jerome says of the Pelagians in his time: 'The discovery of your opinions is the vanquishing of them, your blasphemies appear at the first blush.'[1]

THE NEED FOR HEAVENLY LIGHT

Hence we learn the necessity that the understanding should be grounded in knowledge which is above nature

---

[1] Jerome (c.347-419) in his *Epistle to Ctesiphon*.

for a well-ordered Christian life. There must be light to discover an end beyond nature, because of which we are Christians, and a rule suitable to direct to that end, which is the will of God in Christ, discovering his good pleasure toward us, and our duty towards him. And in virtue of this discovery we do all that we do which may in any way further what we reckon to be true. The eye must first be single, and then the whole body and frame of our conduct will be light (*Matt.* 6:22); otherwise both we and our course of life are nothing but darkness. The whole conduct of a Christian is nothing else but knowledge reduced to will, affection and practice. If the digestion of food in the stomach is not good, the working of the liver cannot be good; so if there is error in the judgment it mars the whole of practice, as an error in the foundation does a building. God will have no blind sacrifices, no unreasonable services (*Isa.* 1:13), but will have us to love him with all our mind (*Rom.* 12:2), that is, with our understanding part, as well as with all our hearts (*Luke* 10:27), that is, the feeling part of the soul.

This ordering of Christ's government by judgment is agreeable to the soul, and God delights to preserve the manner of working peculiar to man, that is, to do what he does out of judgment. As grace supposes nature, as founded upon it, so the frame of grace preserves the frame of nature in man. And, therefore Christ brings about all that is good in the soul through judgment, and that so sweetly that many, by a dangerous error, think that that good which is in them and issues from them is from themselves, and not from the powerful work of grace. So it is in evil, where the devil so subtly leads us according to the stream of our own nature that men think that Satan had no hand in their sin; but here a mistake is with little peril, because we are evil of ourselves, and the devil only promotes ill he finds in us. But there are no seeds of supernatural goodness at all in us. God finds nothing in us but enmity, only he has engraved in our nature an inclination in general to that which we judge to be good. Now when he clearly reveals what is good in particular, we are attracted to it; and when he shows us convincingly what is evil we abhor it as freely as we embraced it before.

From this we may know whether we work as we should do or not. That is, when we do what we do out of inward principles, when we do not choose what is good only because we were so brought up, or because such and such whom we respect do so, or because we will maintain a side, so making religion a faction; but out of judgment, when what we do that is good we first judge in ourselves so to be; and what we abstain from that is ill we first judge to be ill from an inward judgment. A sound Christian, as he enjoys the better part, so has he first made choice of it with Mary (*Luke* 10:42). He establishes every purpose by counsel (*Prov.* 20:18). God, indeed, uses carnal men to very good service, but without a thorough altering and conviction of their judgment. He works by them, but not in them. Therefore they do neither approve the good they do nor hate the evil they abstain from.

WHERE CHRIST'S GOVERNMENT IS SET UP

The second branch of this conclusion is that, wherever true wisdom and judgment are, there Christ has set up his government, because where wisdom is it directs us, not only to understand, but to order our ways aright. Where Christ as a prophet teaches by his Spirit, he likewise as a king subdues the heart by his Spirit to obedience to what is taught. This is that teaching which is promised of God, when not only the brain but the heart itself is taught; when men do not only know what they should do but are taught the very doing of it. They are not only taught that they should love, fear and obey, but they are taught love itself, and fear and obedience themselves. Christ sets up his throne in the very heart and alters its direction, so making his subjects good, together with teaching them to be good. Other princes can make good laws, but they cannot write them in their people's hearts (*Jer.* 31:33). This is Christ's prerogative: he infuses into his subjects his own Spirit. Upon him there does not only rest the spirit of wisdom and understanding, but likewise the spirit of the fear of the Lord (*Isa.* 11:2). The knowledge which we have of him from himself is a transforming knowledge (*2 Cor.* 3:18). The same Spirit who enlightens the mind inspires gracious inclinations into the will and affections and infuses strength into the whole man. As a gracious man judges as he should, so he inclines to and does as he judges. His life is a commentary on his inward man. There is a sweet harmony among God's truth, his judgment, and his whole conversation.

HOW CHRIST GOVERNS US

The heart of a Christian is like Jerusalem when it was at its best, a city compact within itself (*Psa.* 122:3), where are set up the thrones of judgment (*Psa.* 122:5). Judgment should have a throne in the heart of every Christian. Not that judgment alone will work a change. There must be grace to alter the bent and sway of the will before it will yield to be wrought upon by the understanding. But God has so joined these together that whenever he savingly shines on the understanding he gives a soft and pliable heart. For without a work upon the heart by the Spirit of God it will follow its own inclination to that which it loves, whatever the judgment shall say to the contrary. There is no natural proportion between an unsanctified heart and a sanctified judgment. For the unaltered heart will not give leave to the judgment coldly and soberly to conclude what is best, as a sick man, whilst his feverish illness corrupts his taste, is rather desirous to please that than to hearken to what the physician may say. Judgment has no power over itself where the will is unsubdued, for the will and affections bribe it to give sentence for them, when any profit or pleasure shall come in competition with that which the judgment only shall in general think to be good. And therefore it is, for the most part, in the power of the heart what the understanding shall judge and determine in particular things. Where grace has subdued the heart, unruly passions do not cast such a mist before the understanding that it does not see in particular cases what is best. Base considerations, springing from self-love, do not alter the case and bias the judgment into a contrary way; but that which is good in itself shall be good to us, although it crosses our particular worldly interests.

THE EFFECTS OF THIS IN PRACTICE

The right understanding of this has an influence on practice, which has drawn me to a more full explanation. This will teach us the right method of godliness: to begin with judgment, and then to beg of God, together with illumination, holy inclinations of our will and affections, that so a perfect government may be set up in our hearts, and that our knowledge may be 'in all judgment' (*Phil.* 1:9), that is, with experience and feeling. When the judgment of Christ is set up in our judgments, and thence, by the Spirit of Christ, brought into our hearts, then it is in its proper place and throne. Until then, truth does us no good, but helps to condemn us. The life of a Christian is a regular life, and he that walks by the rule (*Gal.* 6:16) of the new creature, peace shall be upon him. He that despises God's way and loves to live at large, seeking all liberty to the flesh, shall die (*Prov.* 19:16). And it is made good by Paul, 'If ye live after the flesh, ye shall die' (*Rom.* 8:13).

We learn likewise that men of an ill-governed life have no true judgment. No wicked man can be a wise man. Without Christ's Spirit the soul is in confusion, without beauty and form, as all things were in the chaos before the creation. The whole soul is out of joint till it be set right again by him whose office is to 'restore all things'. The baser part of the soul, which should be subject, rules all and subdues what little truth is in the understanding, holding it captive to base affections. And Satan by corruption gets all the holds of the soul, till Christ, stronger than he, comes and drives him out, taking possession of all the powers and parts of soul and body to be weapons of righteousness, to serve him. Then it becomes true, 'New lords, new laws'. Christ as a new conqueror changes the fundamental laws of old Adam and establishes a government of his own.

13. *Grace Shall Reign*

The third conclusion from the final part of the text is that Christ's government will be victorious. Let us see the reasons for this.

WHY CHRIST'S KINGDOM MUST PREVAIL

1. Christ has conquered all in his own person first, and he is 'over all, God blessed for ever' (*Rom.* 9:5), and therefore over sin, death, hell, Satan and the world. And, as he has overcome them in himself, so he overcomes them in our hearts and consciences. We commonly say that conscience makes a man kingly or contemptible, because it is planted in us to judge for God, either with us or against us. Now if natural conscience be so forcible, what will it be when, besides its own light, it has the light of divine truth put into it? It will undoubtedly prevail, either to make us hold up our heads with boldness or abase us beneath ourselves. If it subjects itself, by grace, to Christ's truth, then it boldly faces death, hell, judgment and all spiritual enemies, because then Christ sets up his kingdom in the conscience and makes it a kind of paradise.

The sharpest conflict which the soul has is between the conscience and God's justice. Now if the conscience, sprinkled with the blood of Christ, has prevailed over assaults fetched from the justice of God, now satisfied by Christ, it will prevail over all other opposition whatsoever.

2. We are to encounter accursed and damned enemies; therefore, if they begin to fall before the Spirit in us, they shall fall. If they rise up again, it is to have the greater fall.

3. The Spirit of truth, to whose tuition Christ has committed his church, and the truth of the Spirit, which is the sceptre of Christ, abide forever; therefore the soul begotten by the immortal seed of the Spirit (*1 Pet.* 1:23), and this truth, must not only live for ever, but also prevail over all that oppose it, for both the Word and the Spirit are mighty in operation (*Heb.* 4:12). And, if the wicked spirit is never idle in those whom God has delivered up to him, we cannot think that the Holy Spirit will be idle in those whose leading and government is committed to him. No, as he dwells in them, so he will drive out all that rise up against him, until he is all in all.

What is spiritual is eternal. Truth is a beam of Christ's Spirit, both in itself and as it is engrafted into the soul. Therefore it, and the grace wrought by it, though little, will prevail. A little thing in the hand of a giant will do great things. A little faith strengthened by Christ will work wonders.

4. 'Unto everyone that hath shall be given' (*Matt.* 25:29). The victory over corruption or temptation is a pledge of final victory. As Joshua said when he set his foot upon the five kings whom he conquered, 'Thus shall the LORD do to all your enemies' (*Josh.* 10:25). Heaven is ours already, only we strive till we have full possession.

5. Christ as king brings in a commanding light into the soul and bows the neck, and softens the iron sinew of the inner man; and where he begins to rule, he rules for ever, 'of his kingdom there shall be no end' (*Luke* 1:33).

6. The purpose of Christ's coming was to destroy the works of the devil, both for us and in us; and the purpose of the resurrection was, as well as sealing to us the assurance of his victory, so also (1) to quicken our souls from death in sin; (2) to free our souls from such snares and sorrows of spiritual death as accompany the guilt of sin; (3) to raise them up more comfortable, as the sun breaks forth more gloriously out of a thick cloud; (4) to raise us out of particular slips and failings stronger; (5) to raise us out of all troublesome and dark conditions of this life; and (6) at length to raise our bodies out of the dust. For the same power that the Spirit showed in raising Christ, our Head, from the sorrows of death and the lowest degree of his abasement, that power, obtained by the death of Christ from God, now appeased by that sacrifice, the Spirit will show in the church, which is his body, and in every particular member thereof.

And this power is conveyed by faith, by which, after union with Christ in his estates both of humiliation and of exaltation, we see ourselves, not only dead with Christ, but risen and sitting together with him in heavenly places (*Eph.* 2:6). Now we, apprehending ourselves to be dead and risen, and therefore victorious over all our enemies in our Head, and apprehending that his scope in all this is to conform us to himself, we are by this faith changed into his likeness (*2 Cor.* 3:18), and so become conquerors over all our spiritual enemies, as he is, by that power which we derive from him who is the storehouse of all spiritual strength for all his people. Christ at length will fulfil his purpose in us, and faith rests assured of it, and this assurance is very operative, stirring us up to join with Christ in his purposes.

And so, as to the church in general, by Christ it will have its victory. Christ is that little 'stone cut out without hands' which broke in pieces the goodly image (*Dan.* 2:34), that is, all opposite government, until it became 'a great mountain, and filled the whole earth' (*Dan.* 2:35). So that the stone that was cut out of the mountain becomes a mountain itself at length. Who art thou, then, O mountain, that think to stand up against *this* mountain? All shall lie flat and level before it. He will bring down all mountainous, high, exalted thoughts, and lay the pride of all flesh low. When chaff strives against the wind, or stubble against the fire, when the heel kicks against the pricks, when the potsherd strives with the potter, when man strives against God, it is easy to know on which side the victory will be. The winds may toss the ship wherein Christ is, but not overturn it. The waves may dash against the rock, but they only break themselves against it.

WHY THE ENEMY SEEMS VICTORIOUS

Objection: If this is so, why is it thus with the church of God, and with many a gracious Christian? The victory seems to be with the enemy.

To understand this, we should remember, firstly, that God's children usually, in their troubles, overcome by suffering. Here lambs overcome lions, and doves eagles, by suffering, that herein they may be conformable to Christ, who conquered most when he suffered most. Together with Christ's kingdom of patience there was a kingdom of power.

Secondly, this victory is by degrees, and therefore they are too hasty-spirited that would conquer as soon as they strike the first stroke, and be at the end of their race at the first setting forth. The Israelites were sure of their victory in their journey to Canaan, yet they must fight it out. God would not have us quickly forget what cruel enemies Christ has overcome for us. 'Slay them not, lest my people forget,' says the Psalmist (*Psa.* 59:11), so that, by the experience of that annoyance we have by them, we might be kept in fear to come under their power.

Thirdly, God often works by contraries: when he means to give victory, he will allow us to be foiled at first; when he means to comfort, he will terrify first; when he means to justify, he will condemn us first; when he means to make us glorious, he will abase us first. A Christian conquers, even when he is conquered. When he is conquered by some sins, he gets victory over others more dangerous, such as spiritual pride and security.

Fourthly, Christ's work, both in the church and in the hearts of Christians, often goes backward so that it may go forward better. As seed rots in the ground in the winter time, but after comes up better, and the harder the winter the more flourishing the spring, so we learn to stand by falls, and get strength by weakness discovered – *virtutis custos infirmitas* (weakness is the keeper of virtue). We take deeper root by shaking. And, as torches flame brighter by moving, thus it pleases Christ, out of his freedom, in this manner to maintain his government in us. Let us herein labour to exercise our faith, so that it may answer Christ's way of dealing with us. When we are foiled, let us believe we shall overcome; when we have fallen, let us believe we shall rise again. Jacob, after he received a blow which made him lame, yet would not give over wrestling (*Gen.* 32:25) till he had obtained the blessing. So let us never give up, but, in our thoughts, knit the beginning, progress and end together, and then we shall see ourselves in heaven out of the reach of all enemies. Let us assure ourselves that God's grace, even in this imperfect state, is stronger than man's free will in the state of original perfection. It is founded now in Christ, who, as he is the author, so will he be the finisher, of our faith (*Heb.* 12:2). We are under a more gracious covenant.

What some say of rooted faith, *fides radicata*, that it continues, while weak faith may come to nothing, seems to be contradicted by this Scripture; for, as the strongest faith may be shaken, so the weakest, where truth is, is so far rooted that it will prevail. Weakness with watchfulness will stand, when strength with too much confidence fails. Weakness, with acknowledgement of it, is the fittest seat and subject for God to perfect his strength in; for consciousness of our infirmities drives us out of ourselves to him in whom our strength lies.

From this it follows that weakness may be consistent with the assurance of salvation. The disciples, notwithstanding all their weaknesses, are bidden to rejoice that their names are written in heaven (*Luke* 10:20). Failings, with conflict, in sanctification should not weaken the peace of our justification and assurance of salvation. It matters not so much what ill is in us, as what good; not what corruptions, but how we regard them; not what our particular failings are so much as what the thread and tenor of our lives are, for Christ's dislike of that which is amiss in us turns not to the hatred of our persons but to the victorious subduing of all our infirmities.

Some have, after conflict, wondered at the goodness of God that so little and such trembling faith should have upheld them in so great combats, when Satan had almost caught them. And, indeed, it is to be wondered at, how much a little grace will prevail with God for acceptance, and over our enemies for victory, if the heart is upright. Such is the goodness of our sweet Saviour that he delights still to show his strength in our weakness.

CONSOLATION FOR WEAK CHRISTIANS

The first use of this is for the great consolation of poor and weak Christians. Let them know that a spark from heaven, though kindled under greenwood that sobs and smokes, yet it will consume all at last. Love once kindled is strong as death. Many waters cannot quench it, and therefore it is called a vehement flame, or flame of God (*Song of Sol.* 8:6), kindled in the heart by the Holy Ghost. That little that is in us is fed with an everlasting spring. As the fire that came down from heaven in Elijah's time (*1 Kings* 18:38) licked up all the water, to show that it came from God, so will this fire consume all our corruption. No affliction without or corruption within shall quench it. In the morning, we often see clouds gather about the sun, as if they would hide it, but the sun overcomes them little by little, till it comes to its full strength. At first, fears and doubts hinder the breaking out of this fire, until at length it gets above them all, and Christ prevails. And then he upholds his own graces in us. Grace conquers us first, and we, by it, conquer all else; whether corruptions within us, or temptations from outside us.

The church of Christ, begotten by the Word of truth, has the doctrine of the apostles for her crown, and tramples the moon, that is, the world and all worldly things, 'under her feet' (*Rev.* 12:1). Every one that is 'born of God overcometh the world' (*1 John* 5:4). Faith, whereby especially Christ rules, sets the soul so high that it looks down on all other things as far below, as having represented to it, by the Spirit of Christ, riches, honour, beauty and pleasures of a higher nature.

EVIDENCES OF CHRIST'S RULE IN US

Now, that we may not come short of the comfort intended, there are two things especially to be taken notice of by us: firstly, whether there is such a judgment or government set up in us to which this promise of victory is made, and secondly, how we are to conduct ourselves so that the judgment of Christ in us may indeed be victorious.

The evidences whereby we may come to know that Christ's judgment in us is such as will be victorious, are:

1. Being able from experience to justify all Christ's ways, let flesh and blood say what they can to the contrary, and willingly subscribing to that course which God has taken in Christ to bring us to heaven, still approving a further measure of grace than we have attained to, and projecting and planning for it. No other men can justify their courses, when their conscience is awakened.

2. Having reasons of religion the strongest reasons with us, prevailing more than reasons fetched from worldly policy.

3. Being so true to our ends and steadfast to our rule that no hopes or fears can sway us another way, but still we are enquiring what agrees with or differs from our rule.

4. Being able to 'do nothing against the truth, but for the truth' (*2 Cor.* 13:8), the truth being dearer to us than our lives. Truth does not have this sovereignty in the heart of any carnal man.

5. If we had liberty to choose under whose government we would live, out of a delight in the inner man to Christ's government, making choice of him only to rule us before any other. This argues that we are like-minded

to Christ, a free and a willing people, and not compelled to Christ's service otherwise than by the sweet constraint of love. When we are so far satisfied with the government of Christ's Spirit that we are willing to resign up ourselves to him in all things, then his kingdom is come to us, and our wills are brought to his will. It is the bent of our wills that makes us good or ill.

6. Having a well-ordered, uniform life, not consisting of fits and starts, shows a well-ordered heart; as in a clock, when the hammer strikes well, and the hand of the dial points well, it is a sign that the wheels are rightly set.

7. When Christ's will comes into competition with any earthly loss or gain, yet then, in that particular case, having the heart willing to stoop to Christ is a true sign; for the truest trial of the power of grace is in particular cases which touch us most closely, for there our corruption makes the greatest head. When Christ came nearest to home with the young man in the gospel, he lost a disciple of him (*Matt.* 19. 22).

8. Being able to practise duties pleasing to Christ, though contrary to flesh and the course of the world, and being able to overcome ourselves in that evil to which our nature is prone and stands so much inclined, and which agrees to the ruling passion of the times, which others lie enthralled under, such as desire of revenge, hatred of enemies, private ends, etc., this shows that grace in us is above nature, heaven above earth, and will have the victory.

To make this clearer, and help us in our trial, we must know that there are three degrees of victory: first, when we resist though we are foiled; second, when grace gets the better, though with conflict; and third, when all corruption is perfectly subdued. When we have strength only to resist, we may know Christ's government in us will be victorious, because what is said of the devil is true of all our spiritual enemies, 'Resist the devil, and he will flee from you' (*James* 4:7); because 'Greater is he that is in you', who takes the part of his own grace, 'than he that is in the world' (*1 John* 4:4). And if we may hope for victory from bare resistance, what may we not hope for when the Spirit has gained the upper hand?

14. *Means to Make Grace Victorious*

As to directions on how we are to conduct ourselves so that the judgment of Christ in us may indeed be victorious, we must know that, though Christ has undertaken this victory, yet he accomplishes it by training us up to fight his battles. He overcomes in us by making us 'wise unto salvation' (*2 Tim.* 3:15); and, in the measure that we believe Christ will conquer, in that measure we will endeavour by his grace that we may conquer, for faith is an obedient and a wise grace. Christ makes us wise to ponder and weigh things, and to rank and order them accordingly, so that we may make the fitter choice of what is best. Some rules to help us in judging are these:

RULES FOR RIGHT JUDGMENT

We should judge of things as to whether they help or hinder our main purpose; whether they further or hinder our judgment; whether they make us more or less spiritual, and so bring us nearer to the fountain of goodness, God himself; whether they will bring us peace or sorrow at the last; whether they commend us more or less to God, and whether they are the thing in which we shall approve ourselves to him most. We should also judge of things now as we shall do hereafter when the soul shall be best able to judge, as when we are under any public calamity, or at the hour of death, when the soul gathers itself from all other things to itself. We should look back to former experience and see what is most agreeable to it, and what was best in our worst times. If grace is or was best then, it is best now. We should also labour to judge of things as he does who must judge us, and as holy men judge, who are led by the Spirit. More particularly, we should judge according to what those judge that have no interest in any benefit that may come by the thing which is in question; for outward things blind the eyes even of the wise. We see that papists are most corrupt in those things where their honour, ease, or profit is engaged; but in the doctrine of the Trinity, which does not touch on these things, they are sound. But it is not sufficient that judgment is right. It must also be ready and strong.

KEEPING OUR JUDGMENT CLEAR

1. Where Christ establishes his government, he inspires care to keep the judgment clear and fresh, for while the judgment stands straight and firm, the whole frame of the soul continues strong and impregnable. True judgment in us advances Christ, and Christ will advance it. All sin is either from false principles, or ignorance, or thoughtlessness, or unbelief of what is true. By lack of consideration and weakness of assent, Eve lost her hold at first (*Gen.* 3:6). It is good, therefore, to store up true principles in our hearts, and to refresh them often, that, in virtue of them, our affections and actions may be more vigorous. When judgment is fortified, evil finds no entrance, but good things have a side within us to entertain them. While true convincing light continues, we will not do the least ill

of sin for the greatest ill of punishment. 'In vain the net is spread in the sight of any bird' (*Prov.* 1:17). While the soul is kept aloft, there is little danger of snares below. We must lose our high estimation of things before we can be drawn to any sin.

2. And because knowledge and affection mutually help one another, it is good to keep up our affections of love and delight by all sweet inducements and divine encouragements; for what the heart likes best, the mind studies most. Those that can bring their hearts to delight in Christ know most of his ways. Wisdom loves him that loves her. Love is the best entertainer of truth; and when it is not entertained in the love of it (*2 Thess.* 2:10), lovely as it is, it leaves the heart, and will stay no longer. It has been a successful way of corrupting the judgment, to begin by withdrawing love, because, as we love, so we tend to judge. And therefore it is hard to be affectionate and wise in earthly things. But in heavenly things, where there has been a right informing of the judgment before, the more our affections grow, the better and clearer our judgments will be, because our affections, though strong, can never rise high enough to reach the excellency of the things. We see in the martyrs, when the sweet doctrine of Christ had once gained their hearts, it could not be removed again by all the torments the wit of cruelty could devise. If Christ has once possessed the affections, there is no dispossessing of him again. A fire in the heart overcomes all fires without.

3. Wisdom also teaches us where our weakness lies, and our enemy's strength. By this means a jealous fear is stirred up in us, whereby we are preserved; for out of this godly jealousy we keep those provocations, which are active and working, from that which is passive and

catching in us, as we keep fire from powder. Those who wish to hinder the generation of noisome creatures will hinder the conception first, by keeping male and female apart. This jealous care will be much furthered by observing strictly what has helped or hindered a gracious temper in us, and it will make us take heed that we consult not with flesh and blood in ourselves or others. Otherwise, how can we think that Christ will lead us out to victory, when we take counsel with his and our enemies?

4. Christ also makes us careful to use all means by which fresh thoughts and affections may be stirred up and preserved in us. Christ so honours the use of means, and the care he bestows on us, that he ascribes both preservation and victory to our care in keeping ourselves. 'He that is begotten of God keepeth himself' (*1 John* 5:18), though not by himself, but by the Lord, in dependence on him, in the use of means. We are only safe when we wisely make use of all good advantages that we have access to. By going out of God's ways we go out of his government, and so lose our good frame of mind, and find ourselves overspread quickly with a contrary disposition. When we draw near to Christ (*James* 4:8), in his ordinances, he draws near to us.

5. We must keep grace in exercise. It is not sleepy habits, but grace in exercise, that preserves us. While the soul is in some civil or sacred employment, corruptions within us are much suppressed, and Satan's ways of approach to us stopped. The Spirit then has a way open to enlarge his influence in us, and likewise the protection of angels is then closest to us. This course often prevails more against our spiritual enemies than

direct opposition. Christ is in honour bound to maintain those that are in his work.

6. In following all these directions, we must look up to Christ, the quickening Spirit, and make our resolutions in his strength. Though we are exhorted to cleave to the Lord with full purpose of heart (*Acts* 11:23), yet we must pray with David, 'Keep this for ever in the imagination of the thoughts of the heart of thy people, and prepare their heart unto thee' (*1 Chron.* 29:18). Our hearts are of themselves very loose and unsettled. 'Unite my heart to fear thy name' (*Psa.* 86:11), or else, without him, our best purposes will fall to the ground. It is a pleasing request, out of love to God, to beg such a frame of soul from him, that he may take delight in it; and therefore, in the use of all the means, we must send up our desires and complaints to him for strength and help, and then we may be sure that he will 'send forth judgment unto victory'.

7. Lastly, it furthers the state of the soul to know what frame it should be in, that so we may order our souls accordingly. We should always be fit for communion with God, and be heavenly-minded in earthly business, and be willing to be taken off from it to redeem time for better things. We should be ready at all times to depart hence, and to live in such a condition as we would be content to die in. We should have hearts prepared for every good duty, open to all good opportunities, and shut to all temptations, keeping our watch, and being always ready armed. So far as we come short of these things, so far we have just cause to be humbled, and yet we should press forward, so that we may gain more upon ourselves, and make these things more familiar and lovely to us. And

when we find our souls at all declining, it is best to raise them up presently by some awakening meditations, such as of the presence of God, of the strict reckoning we are to make, of the infinite love of God in Christ and the fruits of it, of the excellency of a Christian's calling, of the short and uncertain time of this life, of how little good all those things that steal away our hearts will do us before long, and of how it shall be for ever with us hereafter, as we spend this short time well or ill. The more we make way for such considerations to sink into our hearts, the more we shall rise nearer to that state of soul which we shall enjoy in heaven. When we grow careless of keeping our souls, then God recovers our taste of good things again by sharp crosses. Thus David, Solomon and Samson were recovered. This taste of good things is much easier kept than recovered.

REASONS FOR SEEMING LACK OF PROGRESS

Objection: But, notwithstanding my striving, I seem to remain at a standstill.

1. Grace, as the seed in the parable, grows, we know not how. Yet at length, when God sees fittest, we shall see that all our endeavour has not been in vain. The tree falls upon the last stroke, yet all the strokes help the work forward.

2. Sometimes victory is suspended because some Achan is not found out, or because we are not humble enough, as Israel had the worst against the Benjamites till they fasted and prayed (*Judg.* 20:26); or because we betray our helps, and do not stand on our guard, and do not soon yield to the motions of the Spirit, who puts us in mind always of the best things, if we would regard his prompting. Our own consciences will tell us, if we give

them leave to speak, that some sinful favouring of ourselves is the cause. The way in this case to prevail is, first, to get the victory over the pride of our own nature by taking shame to ourselves, in humble confession to God; and then, secondly, to overcome the unbelief of our hearts by yielding to the promise of pardon; and then, thirdly, in confidence of Christ's assistance, to set ourselves against those sins which have prevailed over us. So prevailing over ourselves, we shall easily prevail over all our enemies, and conquer all conditions we shall be brought into.

ALL SHOULD SIDE WITH CHRIST

The second use of the truth that Christ will have the victory is to establish the fact that the best course for nations and states is to 'kiss the Son' (*Psa.* 2:12), and to embrace Christ and his religion; to side with Christ, and to own his cause in the world. His side will prove the stronger side at last. Happy are we if Christ honours us so much as to use our help to fight his battle 'against the mighty' (*Judg.* 5:23). True religion in a state is as the main pillar of a house and the post of a tent that upholds all. So also for families, let Christ be the chief governor of the family. And let every one be as a house of Christ, to dwell familiarly in, and to rule. Where Christ is, all happiness must follow. If Christ goes, all will go. Where Christ's government, in his ordinances and his Spirit, is, there all subordinate government will prosper. Religion inspires life and grace into all other things. All other virtues without it are but as a fair picture without a head. Where Christ's laws are written in the heart, there all other good laws are best obeyed. None despise man's law but those that despise Christ's first. *Nemo humanam auctoritatem contemnit, nisi qui divinam prius contempsit* (No one despises human authority unless he first despises

[107]

divine authority). Of all persons, a man guided by Christ is the best; and of all creatures in the world, a man guided merely by will and affection, next to the devil, is the worst. The happiness of weaker things stands in being ruled by stronger. It is best for a blind man to be guided by him that has sight. It is best for sheep, and other feckless creatures, to be guided by man. And it is happiest for man to be guided by Christ, because his government is so victorious that it frees us from the fear and danger of our greatest enemies, and tends to bring us to the greatest happiness that our nature is capable of. This should make us rejoice when Christ reigns in us. When Solomon was crowned, the people rejoiced so that the city rang (*1 Kings* 1:45). Much more should we rejoice in Christ our king.

And likewise for those whose souls are dear to us, our endeavour should be that Christ may reign in them also, that they may be baptized by Christ with this fire (*Matt.* 3:11), that these sparks may be kindled in them. Men labour to cherish the spirit and mettle, as they term it, of those they train up, because they think they will have use of it in the manifold affairs and troubles of this life. Oh, but let us cherish the sparks of grace in them; for a natural spirit in great troubles will fail, but these sparks will make them conquerors over the greatest evils.

The third use of the truth of Christ's victory is to observe that if Christ's judgment shall be victorious, then popery, being an opposite frame, set up by the wit of man to maintain stately idleness, must fall. And it is fallen already in the hearts of those on whom the light of Christ has shone. It is a lie, and founded on a lie, on the infallible judgment of a man subject to sin and error. When that which is taken for a principle of truth becomes a principle of error, the more reliance on it, the more danger there is.

15. Christ's Public Triumph

It is not only said that judgment shall be victorious, but that Christ will bring it forth openly to victory. From this we observe that grace will become glory, and come forth into the sight of all. Now Christ conquers, and achieves his own ends, but he does so to some extent invisibly. His enemies in us and outside us seem to prevail. But he will bring forth judgment unto victory, in full view of all. The wicked that now shut their eyes to this shall see it to their torment. It shall not be in the power of subtle men to see or not see what they wish. Christ will have power over their hearts; and as his wrath shall immediately seize upon their souls against their wills, so will he have power over the eyes of their souls, that they may see and know what will increase their misery. Grief shall be fastened to all their senses, and their senses to grief.

Then all the false glosses which they put upon things shall be wiped off. Men are desirous to have the reputation of good, and yet the sweetness of ill; nothing is so cordially opposed by them as that truth which lays them open to themselves and to the eyes of others, their chief care being how to deceive the world and their own consciences. But the time will come when they shall be driven out of this fools' paradise, and the more subtle their manipulation of things has been, the more shall be their shame.

THE OPEN GLORY OF CHRIST IN HIS MEMBERS

Christ, whom God has chosen to set forth the chief glory of his excellencies, is now veiled in relation to his body the church, but he will come before long to be glorious in his saints (*2 Thess.* 1:10), and not lose the clear manifestation of any of his attributes. He will declare to all the world what he is, and then there shall be no glory but that of Christ and his spouse. Those that are as smoking flax now shall then shine as the sun in the firmament (*Matt.* 13:43), and their judgment shall be brought forth as the noonday (*Psa.* 37:6).

The image of God in Adam had a commanding majesty in it, so that all creatures reverenced him. Much more shall the image of God in its perfection command respect from all. Even now there is a secret awe put into the hearts of the greatest towards those in whom they see any grace to shine. So it was that Herod feared John the Baptist; but what will this be in the day of their bringing forth, which is called 'the manifestation of the sons of God' (*Rom.* 8:19)?

There will be more glorious times when the kingdoms of this world shall be the kingdoms of our Lord and of his Christ (*Rev.* 11:15), and he shall reign for ever. Then shall judgment and truth have their victory. Then Christ will plead his own cause. Truth shall no longer be called heresy and schism, nor heresy catholic doctrine. Wickedness shall no longer go masked and disguised. Goodness shall appear in its own lustre, and shine in its own beams. Things shall be what they are, 'for there is nothing covered, that shall not be revealed' (*Matt.* 10:26).

Iniquity shall not be carried on in a mystery any longer. Deep dissemblers that think to hide their counsels from the Lord shall walk no longer invisible as in the clouds. As Christ will not quench the least spark kindled by himself, so will he damp the fairest blaze of goodly appearances which are not from above.

FOLLOW SINCERITY AND TRUTH

If this were believed, men would make more account of sincerity, which alone will give us boldness, and not seek for covers for their shame, confidence in which, as it makes men now more presumptuous, so it will expose them hereafter to the greater shame.

If judgment shall be brought forth to victory, then those that have been ruled by their own deceitful hearts and a spirit of error shall be brought forth to disgrace. The God that has joined grace and truth with honour has joined sin and shame together at last. All the wit and power of man will never be able to sever what God has coupled together. Truth and piety may be trampled upon for a time, but as the two witnesses (*Rev.* 11:11), after they were slain, rose again, and stood upon their feet, so whatever is of God shall at length stand upon its own foundation. There shall be a resurrection, not only of bodies but of reputations. Can we think that he that threw the angels out of heaven will suffer dust and worms' meat to run a contrary course, and to continue always so? No, as truly as Christ is 'King of kings and Lord of lords' (*Rev.* 19:16), so will he dash all those pieces of earth which rise up against him, 'as a potter's vessel' (*Psa.* 2:9). Was there ever anyone fierce against God and prospered (*Job* 9:4)? No, doubtless the wrath of man shall turn to Christ's praise (*Psa.* 76:10). What was said of Pharaoh shall be said of all heady enemies, who would rather lose their souls than their wills, that they are but raised up for Christ to get himself glory in their confusion.

Let us, then, take heed that we follow not the ways of those men whose ends we shall tremble at. There is not a more fearful judgment which can befall the nature of man than to be given up to a reprobate judgment of persons and things, because it comes under a woe: 'Woe unto them that call evil good, and good evil' (*Isa.* 5:20).

How will those be laden with curses another day who abuse the judgment of others by sophistry and flattery, 'deceiving and being deceived' (*2 Tim.* 3:13)? Then the complaint of our first mother Eve will be taken up, but fruitlessly: 'The serpent beguiled me' (*Gen.* 3:13); Satan has deceived me in such and such; sin has deceived me; a foolish heart has deceived me. It is one of the highest points of wisdom to consider on what grounds we venture our souls. Happy men will they be who have, by Christ's light, a right judgment of things, and suffer that judgment to prevail over their hearts.

The souls of most men are drowned in their senses, and carried away with weak opinions, raised from vulgar mistakes and shadows of things. And Satan is ready to enlarge the imagination of outward good and outward ill, and make it greater than it is, and spiritual things less, presenting them through false glasses. And so men, trusting in vanity, vanquish themselves in their own apprehensions. A woeful condition, when both we and that which we highly esteem shall vanish together. And this will be, as truly as Christ's judgment shall come to victory; and in the measure that the vain heart of man has been enlarged to conceive a greater good in the things of this world than there is, by so much the soul shall be enlarged to be more aware of misery when it sees its error. This is the difference between a godly, wise man and a deluded worldling: that which the one now judges to be vain the other shall hereafter feel to be so when it is too late. But this is the vanity of our natures, that though we shun above all things to be deceived and mistaken in present things, yet in the greatest matters of all we are willingly ignorant and misled.

CHRIST ALONE ADVANCES THIS GOVERNMENT

A further conclusion is this, that this government is set up and advanced by Christ alone. He brings judgment to victory. We both fight and prevail 'in the power of his might' (*Eph.* 6:10). We overcome by the Spirit, obtained by 'the blood of the Lamb' (*Rev.* 12:11).

It is he alone who teaches our hands to war and our fingers to fight (*Psa.* 144:1). Nature, as corrupted, favours its own being, and will maintain itself against Christ's government. Nature, simply considered, cannot raise itself above itself to actions which are spiritual and of a higher order and nature. Therefore the divine power of Christ is necessary to carry us above all our own strength, especially in duties in which we meet with greater opposition; for there, not only nature will fail us, but ordinary grace, unless there is a stronger and a new supply. In taking up a burden that is weightier than ordinary, if there is not a greater proportion of strength than weight, the one who undertakes it will lie under the burden; so for every strong encounter there must be a new supply of strength, as in the case of Peter, who, when he was assaulted with a stronger temptation, being not upheld and shored up with a mightier hand, notwithstanding former strength, foully fell (*Matt.* 26:69–74). And being fallen, in our risings up again, it is Christ that must do the work, by (1) removing, or (2) weakening, or (3) suspending opposite hindrances; and (4) by advancing the power of his grace in us, to a further degree than we had before we fell. Therefore when we have fallen, and by falls have been bruised, let us go to Christ immediately to bind us up again.

WE MUST NOT LOOK TO OURSELVES

Let us know, therefore, that it is dangerous to look for that from ourselves which we must have from Christ. Since the fall, all our strength lies in him, as Samson's in his hair (*Judg.* 16:17). We are but subordinate agents, moving as we are moved, and working as we are first wrought upon, free in so far as we are freed, no wiser nor stronger than he makes us to be for the present in anything we undertake. It is his Spirit who actuates and enlivens, and applies that knowledge and strength we have, or else it fails and lies useless in us. We work when we work from a present strength; therefore dependent spirits are the wisest and the ablest. Nothing is stronger than humility, which goes out of itself, or weaker than pride, which rests on its own foundation. *Frustra nititur qui non innititur* (He strives in vain who is not dependent). And this should be particularly observed because naturally we aspire to a kind of divinity, in setting about actions in the strength of our own abilities; whereas Christ says, 'Without me ye', the apostles, who were in a state of grace, 'can do nothing' (*John* 15:5). He does not say, you can do a little, but nothing. Of ourselves, how easily are we overcome! How weak we are to resist! We are as reeds shaken with every wind. We shake at the very noise and thought of poverty, disgrace or losses. We give in immediately. We have no power over our eyes, tongues, thoughts or affections, but let sin pass in and out. How soon we are overcome by evil, whereas we should overcome evil with good. How many good purposes stick in the birth, and have no strength to come forth – all which shows that we are nothing without the Spirit of Christ. We see how weak the apostles themselves were, till they were endued with strength from above. Peter was blasted with the speech of a damsel (*Matt.* 20:69), but after the Spirit of Christ fell upon them, the more they suffered, the more they were encouraged to suffer. Their comforts grew with their troubles. Therefore in all, especially difficult encounters, let us lift up our hearts to Christ, who has Spirit enough for us all, in all our exigencies, and say with good Jehoshaphat, 'We have no might . . . neither know we what to do: but our eyes are upon thee' (*2 Chron.* 20:12); the battle we fight is thine, and the strength whereby we fight must be thine. If thou goest not out with us, we are sure to be foiled. Satan knows that nothing can prevail against Christ, or those that rely upon his power. Therefore his study is how to keep us in ourselves, and in the creature. But we must carry this always in our minds, that that which is begun in self-confidence ends in shame.

CHRIST MAKES US FEEL OUR DEPENDENCE

The manner of Christ's bringing forth judgment to victory is by letting us see a necessity of dependence on him. Hence proceed those spiritual desertions in which he often leaves us to ourselves, in regard to both grace and comfort, that we may know the spring-head of these to be outside ourselves. Hence it is that in the mount, that is, in extremities, God is most seen (*Gen.* 22:14). Hence it is that we are saved by the grace of faith which carries us out of ourselves to rely upon another; and faith works best alone, when it has least outward support. Hence it is that we often fail in lesser conflicts and stand firm in greater, because in the lesser we rest more in ourselves, in the greater we fly to the rock of our salvation, which is higher than we (*Psa.* 61:2). Hence also it is that we are stronger after defeats, because hidden corruption, undiscerned before, is now discovered, and thence we are brought to make use of mercy pardoning and power supporting.

One main reason for this dispensation is that we should know it is Christ that gives both the will and the deed, and that as a voluntary work according to his own good pleasure. And therefore we should work out our salvation in a jealous fear and trembling (*Phil.* 2:12), lest by irreverent and presumptuous conduct we give him cause to suspend his gracious influence and leave us to the darkness of our own hearts.

THE TRIUMPH OF GRACE

Those that are under Christ's government have the spirit of revelation, whereby they see and feel a divine power sweetly and strongly enabling them to preserve faith when they feel the contrary, and hope in a state which is hopeless, and love to God under signs of his displeasure, and heavenly-mindedness in the midst of worldly affairs and allurements which draw a contrary way. They feel a power preserving patience, nay joy, in the midst of causes of mourning, inward peace in the midst of assaults. Whence is it that, when assaulted with temptation and compassed with troubles, we have stood firm, but from a secret strength upholding us? To make so little grace so victorious over so great a mass of corruption, this requires a spirit more than human. This is like preserving fire in the sea, and a part of heaven even, as it were, in hell. Here we know where to obtain this power, and to whom to return the praise of it. And it is our happiness that it is so safely hid in Christ for us, in one so near to God and us. Since the fall, God will not trust us with our own salvation, but it is both purchased and kept by Christ for us, and we for it through faith, wrought by the power of God, which we lay hold of. This power is gloriously set forth by Paul: it is (1) a great power; (2) an exceeding power; (3) a working and a mighty power; (4) such a power as was wrought in raising Christ from the dead (*Eph.* 1:19–20). That grace which is but a persuasive offer and in our power to receive or refuse is not the grace which brings us to heaven. But God's people feel a powerful work of the Spirit, not only revealing to us our misery and deliverance through Christ, but emptying us of ourselves, as being redeemed from ourselves, and infusing new life into us, and afterwards strengthening us and quickening us when we droop and hang the wing, never leaving us till the conquest is perfect.

16. *Through Conflict to Victory*

The text also implies that the prevailing of Christ's government will not be without fighting. There can be no victory where there is no combat. In Isaiah it is said, 'He shall bring forth judgment unto truth' (*Isa.* 42:3). In Matthew it is said that he shall 'send forth judgment unto victory' (*Matt.* 12:20). The word 'send forth' has a stronger sense in the original: to send forth with force; showing that, where his government is in truth, it will be opposed, until he gets the upper hand. Nothing is so opposed as Christ and his government are, both within us and outside us; and within us most in our conversion. Though corruption does not prevail so far as to make void the powerful work of grace, yet there is not only a possibility of opposing, but a proneness to oppose, and not only a proneness, but an actual withstanding of the working of Christ's Spirit, and that in every action. Yet there is no prevailing resistance so far as to make void the work of grace, but corruption in the issue yields to grace.

It takes much trouble to bring Christ into the heart, and to set up a tribunal for him to judge there. There is an army of lusts in mutiny against him. The utmost strength of most men's endeavours and abilities is directed to keeping Christ from ruling in the soul. The flesh still labours to maintain its own government, and therefore it cries down the credit of whatever crosses it, such as God's blessed ordinances, and highly prizes anything, though never so dead and empty, if it allows the liberty of the flesh.

WHY CHRIST'S GOVERNMENT IS OPPOSED

And no marvel if the spiritual government of Christ is so opposed:

First, because it is *government,* and that limits the course of the will and casts a bridle on its wanderings. Everything natural resists what opposes it; so the corrupt will labours to bear down all laws, and counts it a noble thing not to be awed, and an argument of a low spirit to fear any, even God himself, until unavoidable danger seizes on men. Then those that feared least when out of danger fear most in danger, as we see in the case of Belshazzar (*Dan.* 5:6).

Secondly, it is *spiritual government,* and therefore the flesh will endure it even less. Christ's government brings the very thoughts and desires, which are the most immediate and free issue of the soul, into obedience. Though a man were of such controlled behaviour that his whole life were free from outward offences, yet in Christ's eyes to be carnally or worldly-minded is death (*Rom.* 8:6). He looks on a worldly mind with a greater detestation than any one particular offence.

One may say, 'But Christ's Spirit is in those who are in some degree earthly-minded.' True, but not as an allower and maintainer, but as an opposer, subduer, and in the end as a conqueror. Carnal men would like to

[119]

bring Christ and the flesh together, and could be content, with some reservation, to submit to Christ. But Christ will be no underling to any base affection, and therefore, where there is allowance of ourselves in any sinful lust, it is a sign the keys were never given up to Christ to rule us.

Thirdly, this judgment is opposed, because it is *judgment*, and men do not like to be judged and censured. Now Christ, in his truth, arraigns them, gives sentence against them, and binds them over to the latter judgment of the great day, and therefore they take upon them to judge that truth which must judge them. But truth will be too strong for them. Man has a day now, which Paul calls 'man's day' (*1 Cor.* 4:3 *[margin]*), in which he gets on his bench and usurps a judgment over Christ and his ways; but God has a day in which he will set everything straight, and his judgment shall stand. And the saints shall have their time, when they shall sit in judgment on those that judge them now (*1 Cor.* 6:2). In the meantime, Christ will rule in the midst of his enemies (*Psa.* 110:2), even in the midst of our hearts.

WE MUST EXPECT OPPOSITION

It is therefore no sign of a good condition to find all quiet, with no opposition; for can we think that corruption, which is the older element in us, and Satan, the strong man who has many holds over us, will yield possession quietly? No, there is not so much as a thought of goodness discovered by him, but he joins with corruption to kill it in the birth. And as Pharaoh's cruelty was especially against the male children, so Satan's malice is especially against the most religious and manly resolutions.

This, then, we are always to expect, that wherever Christ comes there will be opposition. When Christ was born, all Jerusalem was troubled; so when Christ is born in any man, the soul is in an uproar, and all because the heart is unwilling to yield up itself to Christ to rule it.

Wherever Christ comes he brings division, not only between man and himself, but between man and man, and between church and church; of which disturbance Christ is no more the cause than medicine is of trouble in a diseased body. Harmful agents are the real cause, for the purpose of medicine is to bring health. But Christ thinks it fit that the thoughts of men's hearts should be revealed, and he is set for the fall as well as the rising of many in Israel (*Luke* 2:34).

Thus the desperate madness of men is laid open, that they would rather be under the guidance of their own lusts, and in consequence of Satan himself, to their endless destruction, than put their feet into Christ's fetters and their necks under his yoke; though, indeed, Christ's service is the only true liberty. His yoke is an easy yoke, his burden but as the burden of wings to a bird which make her fly the higher. Satan's government is rather a bondage than a government, to which Christ gives up those that shake off his own, for then he gives Satan and his agents power over them. Since they will not 'receive the love of the truth' (*2 Thess.* 2:10), take him, Jesuit, take him, Satan, blind him and bind him and lead him to perdition. Those that take the most liberty to sin are the greatest slaves, because the most voluntary slaves. The will is either the best or the worst part in anything. The further men go on in a wilful course, the deeper they sink in rebellion; and the more they oppose Christ, doing what they will, the more they shall one day suffer what they would not. In the meantime, they are prisoners in their own souls, bound over in their consciences to the judgment after death of him whose judgment they would not accept in their lives. And is it not just that they should find him a severe judge to condemn them when they would not have him as a mild judge to rule them?

OUR VICTORY IN CHRIST IS CERTAIN

In conclusion and as a general application to ourselves of all that has been said, we see the conflicting, but yet sure and hopeful, state of God's people. The victory lies not with us, but with Christ, who has taken on him both to conquer for us and to conquer in us. The victory lies neither in our own strength to get it, nor in our enemies' strength to defeat it. If it lay with us, we might justly fear. But Christ will maintain his own government in us and take our part against our corruptions. They are his enemies as well as ours. Let us therefore be 'strong in the Lord, and in the power of his might' (*Eph.* 6:10). Let us not look so much at who our enemies are as at who our judge and captain is, nor at what they threaten, but at what he promises. We have more for us than against us. What coward would not fight when he is sure of victory? None is here overcome but he that will not fight. Therefore, when any base fainting seizes on us, let us lay the blame where it ought to be laid.

Discouragement rising from unbelief and the ill report brought upon the good land by the spies moved God to swear in his wrath that they should not enter into his rest. Let us take heed that a spirit of faint-heartedness, rising from the seeming difficulty and disgrace involved in God's good ways, does not provoke God to keep us out of heaven. We see here what we may look for from heaven. O beloved, it is a comfortable thing to conceive of Christ aright, to know what love, mercy and strength we have laid up for us in the breast of Christ. A good opinion of the physician, we say, is half the cure. Let us make use of this mercy and power of his every day in our daily combats: 'Lord Jesus, thou hast promised not to quench the smoking flax, nor to break the bruised reed. Cherish thy grace in me; leave me not to myself; the glory shall be thine.' Let us not allow Satan to transform Christ to us, to make him other than he is to those that are his. Christ will not leave us till he has made us like himself, all glorious within and without, and presented us blameless before his Father (*Jude* 24).

What a comfort this is in our conflicts with our unruly hearts, that it shall not always be thus! Let us strive a little while, and we shall be happy for ever. Let us think when we are troubled with our sins that Christ has this in charge from his Father, that he shall not 'quench the smoking flax' until he has subdued all. This puts a shield into our hands to beat back 'all the fiery darts of the wicked' (*Eph.* 6:16). Satan will object, 'You are a great sinner.' We may answer, 'Christ is a strong Saviour.' But he will object, 'You have no faith, no love.' 'Yes, a spark of faith and love.' 'But Christ will not regard that.' 'Yes, he will not quench the smoking flax.' 'But this is so little and weak that it will vanish and come to nought.' 'Nay, but Christ will cherish it, until he has brought judgment to victory.' And this much we have already for our comfort, that, even when we first believed, we overcame God himself, as it were, by believing the pardon of all our sins, notwithstanding the guilt of our own consciences and his absolute justice. Now, having been prevailers with God, what shall stand against us if we can learn to make use of our faith?

Oh, what a confusion is this to Satan, that he should labour to blow out a poor spark and yet should not be able to quench it; that a grain of mustard seed should be stronger than the gates of hell; that it should be able to remove mountains of oppositions and temptations cast up by Satan and our rebellious hearts between God and us. Abimelech could not endure that it should be said, 'A woman slew him' (*Judg.* 9:54); and it must needs be a torment to Satan that a weak child, a woman, a decrepit old man should, by a spirit of faith, put him to flight.

TREASURE THE LEAST DEGREE OF GRACE

Since there is such comfort where there is a little truth of grace, that it will be so victorious, let us often try what God has wrought in us, search our good as well as our ill, and be thankful to God for the least measure of grace, more than for any outward thing. It will be of more use and comfort than all this world which passes away and comes to nothing. Yea, let us be thankful for that promised and assured victory which we may rely on without presumption, as Paul does: 'But thanks be to God, which giveth us the victory through our Lord Jesus Christ' (*1 Cor.* 15:57). See a flame in a spark, a tree in a seed. See great things in little beginnings. Look not so much to the beginning as to the perfection, and so we shall be, in some degree, joyful in ourselves, and thankful to Christ.

Neither must we reason from a denial of a great measure of grace to a denial of any at all in us, for faith and grace do not consist in an indivisible amount, so that he who has not such and such a measure has none at all. But, as there is a great difference between a spark and a flame, so there is a great difference between the least measure of grace and the greatest; and he who has the least measure is within the compass of God's eternal favour. Though he is not a shining light, yet he is a smoking wick, which Christ's tender care will not allow him to quench.

ENCOURAGEMENT TO COME TO CHRIST

And let all that has been spoken allure those that are not yet in a state of grace to come under Christ's sweet and victorious government, for, though we shall have much opposition, yet, if we strive, he will help us. If we fail, he will cherish us. If we are guided by him, we shall overcome. If we overcome, we are sure to be crowned. As for the present state of the church, we see now how forlorn it is, yet let us comfort ourselves that Christ's cause shall prevail. Christ will rule, till his enemies become his footstool (*Psa.* 110:1), not only to trample upon, but to help him up to mount higher in glory. Babylon shall fall, 'for strong is the Lord God who judgeth her' (*Rev.* 18:8). Christ's judgment, not only in his children, but also against his enemies, shall be victorious, for he is 'King of kings and Lord of lords' (*Rev.* 19:16). God will not always suffer antichrist and his supporters to revel and swagger in the church as they do.

CHRIST IS THE HOPE OF THE CHURCH

If we look to the present state of the church of Christ, it is as Daniel in the midst of lions, as a lily amongst thorns, as a ship not only tossed but almost covered with waves. It is so low that the enemies think they have buried Christ, with respect to his gospel, in the grave, and there they think to keep him from rising. But as Christ rose in his person, so he will roll away all stones and rise again in his church. How little support has the church and cause of Christ at this day! How strong a conspiracy is against it! The spirit of antichrist is now lifted up and marches furiously. Things seem to hang on a small and invisible thread. But our comfort is that Christ lives and reigns, and stands on Mount Zion in defence of those who stand for him (*Rev.* 14:1); and when states and kingdoms shall dash one against another Christ will have care of his own children and cause, seeing there is nothing else in the world that he much esteems. At this very time the delivery of his church and the ruin of his enemies are in progress. We see nothing in motion till Christ has done his work, and then we shall see that the Lord reigns.

Christ and his church, when they are at the lowest, are nearest rising. His enemies, at the highest, are nearest their downfall. The Jews are not yet come in under Christ's banner; but God who has persuaded Japheth to come into the tents of Shem (*Gen.* 9:27) will persuade Shem to come into the tents of Japheth. The 'fulness of the Gentiles' has not yet come in (*Rom.* 11:25), but Christ, who has the uttermost parts of the earth given to him for his possession (*Psa.* 2:8), will gather all the sheep his Father has given him into one fold, that there may be one sheepfold and one shepherd (*John* 10:16). The faithful Jews rejoiced to think of the calling of the Gentiles and why should we not rejoice to think of the calling of the Jews?

The gospel's course has hitherto been as that of the sun, from east to west, and so in God's time it may proceed yet further west. No creature can hinder the course of the sun, nor stop the influence of heaven, nor hinder the blowing of the wind, much less hinder the prevailing power of divine truth, until Christ has brought all under one head, and then he will present all to his Father: 'These are those thou hast given to me; these are those that have taken me for their Lord and King, that have suffered with me. My will is that they may be where I am and reign with me.' And then he will deliver up the kingdom, even to his Father, and put down all other rule, and authority, and power (*1 Cor.* 15:24).

FAITH WILL PREVAIL

Let us then bring our hearts to holy resolutions, and set ourselves upon that which is good, and against that which is ill, in ourselves or others, according to our callings, with this encouragement, that Christ's grace and power will go along with us. What would have become of that great work of reformation of religion in the latter-spring of the gospel if men had not been armed with invincible courage to overcome all hindrances, with this faith, that the cause was Christ's, and that he would not fail to help his own cause? Luther ingenuously confessed that he often acted inconsiderately and moved by various passions. But when he acknowledged this, God did not condemn him for his errors, but, the cause being God's, and his aims being holy, to promote the truth, and being a mighty man in prayer, and strong in faith, God by him kindled that fire which all the world shall never be able to quench. According to our faith, so is our encouragement to all duties, therefore let us strengthen faith, so that it may strengthen all other graces. The very belief that faith shall be victorious is a means to make it so indeed. Believe it, therefore, that, though it is often as smoking flax, yet it shall prevail. If it prevails with God himself in trials, shall it not prevail over all other opposition? Let us wait a while, 'stand still, and see the salvation of the LORD' (*Exod.* 14:13).

The Lord reveal himself more and more to us in the face of his Son Jesus Christ and magnify the power of his grace in cherishing those beginnings of grace in the midst of our corruptions, and sanctify the consideration of our own infirmities to humble us, and of his tender mercy to encourage us. And may he persuade us that, since he has taken us into the covenant of grace, he will not cast us off for those corruptions which, as they grieve his Spirit, so they make us vile in our own eyes. And because Satan labours to obscure the glory of his mercy and hinder our comfort by discouragements, the Lord add this to the rest of his mercies, that, since he is so gracious to those that yield to his government, we may make the right use of this grace, and not lose any portion of comfort that is laid up for us in Christ. And may he grant that the prevailing power of his Spirit in us should be an evidence of the truth of grace begun, and a pledge of final victory, at that time when he will be all in all, in all his, for all eternity. Amen.